I0023421

NO CONTRACEPTION NO DOLE

TACKLING INTERGENERATIONAL WELFARE

GARY JOHNS

connorcourt
PUBLISHING

Connor Court Publishing Pty Ltd

PO Box 224W
Ballarat VIC 3350
sales@connorcourt.com
www.connorcourt.com

ISBN: 9781925138665 (pbk)

Printed in Australia

Front cover by Ian James

Contents

Tables and figures

Foreword

This book has the power to confront and offend all those who read it: and you should read it.

Some may take offense at the superficial; the title. Some may oppose the central idea that Gary proposes.

Others may find the substantive content, the facts, statistics and case studies, alarming and provoking. There is no doubt this book starts a difficult conversation, and everyone will have a different opinion, but this is a conversation we need to have.

As you progress through, expect to feel disbelief, sadness, and deep outrage. You may ask yourself, as a member of this society what parts have I unwittingly played in these disasters, and what now, is my responsibility to remedy them? We live in a rich country, we want to assist each other in times of need, but this book caused me to wonder whether a line has been crossed, whether in some households the family has been supplanted by the state and whether the state is the worst possible family to have.

You will feel anguish for the children. They are the innocent parties here, they don't ask to be born and when they arrive they deserve the best life we can offer.

Gary's proposal is simple.

He proposes that meaningful conversations occur, between the relevant people at the right time, and that following this, certain obligations are exchanged for real assistance. Gary contends that prevention is better than the cure. I agree with this, and I couldn't think of any better solutions to the challenges this book presents us with, but you might be able to. If this is the case, then the most helpful thing you can do is to add your voice to the conversation and put your ideas forward.

Grace Collier

Other works by the author

Aboriginal Self-determination: The Whiteman's dream

The Charity Ball: how to dance to the donors' tune

Right Social Justice: better ways to help the poor

Recognise What?
Arguments to acknowledge Aborigines, but not recognise Aboriginal culture or rights, in the Australian constitution

Really Dangerous Ideas: what does and does not matter

available from: **www.connorcourt.com**

Dedication

To those dealt a bad hand in life, in the hope of a better life, and to the taxpayers who, unwittingly, may have helped those dealt a bad hand, make bad choices.

Acknowledgements

There are many whom I wish to thank in helping this project. A great many front-line troops such as police, social workers and lawyers who deal with families in difficulty were very encouraged by the original article on which the book is based and very encouraging in the anticipated debate, which the book should generate.

In particular, I have benefited from comments by my friends and colleagues Grace Collier, Jennifer Oriel and Kerryn Pholi. As always, my good friend and editor John Nethercote has edited the book and thanks again to Dr Anthony Cappello of Connor Court for his succour and comfort to right thinking authors. I want to especially thank the Hon Melinda Pavey MP Member for Oxley in the NSW parliament for her encouragement.

I would also like to thank and congratulate the new Minister for Social Security, the Hon Christian Porter, for making available previously unpublished data of estimates of the number of children born to a woman while she is on a benefit. This is the decent thing to do to inform public debate on a sensitive issue.

Elsewhere, I have relied on the latest and best research, especially statistics from a number of long-run Australian and international studies. Statistics are important to confirm the facts, but stories convey the real cost of dependence and the complexity of lives, families and generations involved in welfare.

Children's courts in every Australian state and territory deal with the awful business of youth crime, child abuse or other serious family disputes involving children, many of which result in children being taken into care. We should take our hats off to the officers of the court and other professionals who deal with these matters.

Unfortunately, few children's court cases are reported. The major exception is where a child has died at the hands of a parent or guardian or in care, when a coroner's report is published. Other courts, notably the Family Court of Australia, publish decisions that provide similar insights into family circumstances. I have had access to some cases still in progress and not available to the public. In reporting these, I have made sure that those concerned cannot be identified.

These cases convey the depth of the problem, but they do not suggest that every family, or every family that has issues with parenting or drugs or multiple partners, is doomed. The cases illustrate the severity of the consequences for those families that have been unable to rise above their circumstances. All are or have been welfare dependent.

In February this year, I applied to the Chief Magistrate of Queensland, who is responsible for the Children's Court in Queensland, for access to court files for research purposes. Following his advice I sought and received ethical clearance for the research from the Queensland University of Technology, where I am a visiting fellow. I was thereafter referred to the head of the Queensland Attorney General's Department for permission to access the files. Despite numerous discussions, and providing absolute assurances to anonymity of persons involved in children's court proceedings, permission, while not denied, failed to materialise before the publication date, an eight-month delay. This is a pathetic response from government officials.

Brisbane, October 2015

To bring a child into existence without a fair prospect of being able, not only to provide food for its body, but instruction and training for its mind, is a moral crime, both against the unfortunate offspring and against society; and that if the parent does not fulfil this obligation, the State ought to see it fulfilled, at the charge, as far as possible, of the parent.

J. S. Mill, *On Liberty* 1869

Will there be enough policy levers if it is not all about income or education?

Deborah Cobb-Clark , *Income-support and outcomes of Australian youth* 2010

Most developed societies now support impoverished single mothers, replacing husbands with the state.

Alison Wolf, *The xx factor: how working women are creating a new society* 2013

The old norm was 'don't have a child outside of marriage'. The new norm should be 'don't have a child before you want one and are ready to be a parent'.

Isabel Sawhill, *Generation unbound: drifting into sex and parenthood without marriage* 2014

1

Some Australian women and children are cash cows

It is rough out there

This project started on 27 December 2014, after I read the horrible news that a mother had murdered seven of her children and one other child. The dead numbered three of the mother's girls, aged 12, 11 and two; four of her boys, aged nine, eight, six and five. The eighth victim, a 14-year-old niece, had been staying with them at their home in Cairns.[1] Subsequent enquiries have revealed that the woman had her children to four different fathers. Her income came from you and me, taxpayers. Did anyone ever think to call a halt to this woman and these children being used by men as cash cows?

A couple, refugees to Australia, arrived with one child. They subsequently had seven children. At no time did the mother or father work and they have now separated. A dispute about the care of the children, with taxpayer support, is presently a matter before the Family Court of Australia.[2] All the children have been taken by the relevant state department and placed with the father. The father accused the mother of abusing the children. How does a nation allow such events to occur?

A mother and two fathers are in a children's court in Australia at present fighting a state government department over the long-term guardianship of four children. The mother has had six children to the two fathers, three to each. The mother is on a disability pension and is in supported accommodation. All six children are in care. One father

---

1 Jamie Walker and Sarah Elks, 'Cairns deaths: A "good mum" who concealed her demons.' *The Australian* 27 December 2014.
2 The author attended the court proceedings; the judgement was not available at the time of publication.

is a homeless alcoholic and is on a disability pension; the other was imprisoned for an indictable offence of a most serious nature. The de facto partner of father number two has five children to at least two fathers. Four of those children are subject to child protection orders. At one point the ex-prisoner had the care of one of his children and one of the other father's children. What hope for these children?[3]

In June 2015, an employee working among women in a gaol in the mid-coast of NSW, whose job was to prepare women for release into the community, informed me that some women wanted their 'rod' removed so that they could have a baby after release. A 'rod' is the local name for a Long Acting Reversible Contraceptive (LARC). In all likelihood, the women had no job to go to, just a man who, in all likelihood, had no job. Perhaps the women wanted to be loved or have someone to love, or to be a mother in lieu of anything else, but why would taxpayers knowingly pay for this choice?

Shockingly, I learned from a women's refuge worker in the same region that men had been known to 'flick out' the rod with a knife. They wanted to impregnate the woman. It was unlikely they were expressing a desire to have a family for the love of the child. I venture that it was for the money that came with the woman and the child. There are 1,743 women of childbearing age in Australian gaols.[4] This population may benefit more than most from a form of intervention that prevents them from becoming a cash cow.

A very senior police officer informed me that there was a 26-year-old grandmother living in the mid coast of NSW. A child begets a child and, almost certainly, taxpayers paid for it. The same officer informs me that one man in the region aged in his 50s boasts of siring 21 children. Some men use some women and children as cash cows.

Most women want a child for love, but others want a child for money. Some women use children as cash cows. Ashlee Polkinghorne killed her four year-old daughter Chloe. At the inquest, the State Coroner of South Australia recalled:

When Ashlee became pregnant [her mother] spoke to her about her

3 The judgement was not available at the time of publication.
4 Australian Bureau of Statistics (2014), *Prisoners in Australia, 2014*, table 3.

future and how she would cope with a child. [She] suggested that Ashlee consider a termination, but Ashlee refused to do so and was angry at the suggestion. Ashlee told [her mother] that she wanted someone to love her (State Coroner, 2014, 71).

He concluded:

Chloe represented nothing more to Ashlee than a means by which her income could be enhanced by obtaining support payments not available to a childless person (State Coroner, 2014, 143).

He recommended:

In my opinion it would be reasonable for the Children's Protection Act 1993 to be amended ... by providing that a child born to a person who has a conviction in respect of a child previously born to them for manslaughter ... be placed from birth under the custody of the Minister (State Coroner, 2014, 145).

This strikes me as strange. Why amend an Act of Parliament to ensure a subsequent child of a convicted killer is taken from the mother; if the mother were on welfare, why not prevent the birth of the child? Why not an ounce of prevention to save a pound of cure? Take a recent case, an appeal by a mother against a decision granting long-term guardianship of her child B to the Queensland Department of Communities. The woman was 38 years of age and had nine children, eight of whom were subject to some form of child protection. B had been placed with carers since birth. The woman was caring for B's younger sister N with support [although that child also spent time in care]. It was the opinion of the court that the woman did not have the cognitive capacity to parent two children.

B's father, aged 29, was not able to care for B. The mother had ceased contact with the father in obtaining a domestic violence order. There was a significant domestic violence incident in 2009, which resulted in the appellant being admitted to hospital. She was pregnant with B at the time. The father was gaoled as a consequence. In 2011 the woman tried to rekindle the relationship but the father apparently hit her again.

The child protection history is one of chronic neglect, unhygienic living conditions, inadequate supervision of the children, failure to provide the children's basic necessities and access medical treatment, domestic violence and harmful parenting behaviours. The woman had had 'issues with alcohol' and, although there was a period of stable employment, she was, at the time of the court case, a full-time primary carer of N. The woman told her counsellor that 'past relationships were too hastily formed and based on misjudgement of the men involved'. The father's new partner was pregnant with twins (Children's Court Queensland, 2014).

Taking children is too late ...

In 2012-13, in Australia, there were 135,000 children receiving child protection services – investigation, care and protection orders and/or in out-of-home care. More than half these children were subject only to an investigation (AIHW (b), 2014, viii). Of these, 91,000 were the subject of an investigation, 52,000 were on a care and protection order and 50,000 were in out-of-home care (children may be involved in more than one component of the system). On an average day in 2012-13 there were 32,469 children on a care and protection order. It may be that the parents of only some of these children were on benefits. For example, 65 per cent of children in protective services come from the most disadvantaged groups, but seven per cent come from the most advantaged group (AIHW (b), 2014, 10, 33, 77).

In 2013-14, there were 81,000 children's court cases lodged in Australia, shown in table 1.1. The matters that come before children's courts in Australia are either for the care of children or where the child has committed a criminal offence, and is too young to be dealt with in open court.

Table 1.1. Children's court lodgements, Australia, 2013-14

Children's court	NSW	Vic	Qld	WA	SA	Tas	ACT	NT	Total
Lodgements									
Criminal	9900	20000	12000	6400	5100	1300	300	2100	57100
Civil	8900	7000	3500	2600	1100	300	100	400	23900
Total	18800	27000	15500	9000	6200	1600	400	2500	81000

Sources: (Productivity Commission, 2015, tables 7.2,3,5,6)

Estimates of the incidence of abuse suffered by Australians as a child range from five per cent to 15 per cent of the population. The long-term impacts of child abuse are very large because child abuse is associated with increased numbers of long-term physical and mental health conditions (Segal, 2011, 275). For example, annual adult health care costs of people who were both physically and sexually abused as children was $1,856 greater than those who were not (Reeve, 2013, 311). In 2012-13, the national recurrent expenditure on child protection and out-of-home care services was about $3.2 billion (AIHW (b), 2014, 2).

Australian governments spend billions of taxpayer's dollars to help those who cannot help themselves and billions of taxpayer's dollars on those who need help to raise their children. The interventions are many, including some that are severe, such as taking children from their parents. And yet policy-makers are reluctant to intervene at the earliest point, before conception. They refuse to intervene when they have someone's undivided attention, that is, when they want taxpayer's money. Each of these women could be assisted to delay childbearing until they are in a strong position to do so. These women are unable to rely on their partner, or partners, but it is foolish for government to step in as father. Better it steps in as a friend and wise counsel to protect women from having a child when they are not in a position to support the child.

Female (and male) taxpayers are subsidising the choices of some women to continue having children whilst on welfare, when these taxpayers may not be able to afford to start a family. Money has always been a factor in women's fertility, but why should some women be excused from these financial constraints at the expense of other women? Working women on low incomes often live in outer suburbs and low-cost housing areas where the worst effects of the social chaos of intergenerational welfare are most keenly felt. How is this fair?

It is not a fruitful exercise to seek to blame any one, person or institution, for the fact that some children are born to a parent or parents who cannot care for them. Knowing that some are at greater risk than others of being poorly cared for should be enough, however, to start a fresh search for preventive measures. Knowing that welfare recipients are more likely to parent children who will experience difficulties and may themselves parent children while on welfare provides a big clue as to when and how to intervene. The objective is to give those people the best chance to grow and raise a family that is more likely to succeed free from welfare.

No contraception, no dole

The publication in *The Australian* newspaper of the article, 'No contraception, no dole', on 30 December 2014, caused a minor tsunami in current affairs commentary. In addition to 500 comments received on *The Australian* newspaper's website, there were more than 432,000 'shares', which means that a huge number of readers wanted others to read it. And they did. At least 1.5 million individuals did so. Clearly, and for whatever reasons, many Australians are seriously worried about intergenerational welfare: the phenomenon that people who have children while on welfare are more likely to do so if they come from a family which has been on welfare.

Australian children who grow up in welfare-dependent families are much more likely to be dependent upon welfare as adults (Pech, 2000). Many bright and tenacious children break free and succeed. Many do not. Separation and joblessness are two major causes of dependence. Both are intergenerational. Children, whose grandparents or parents experienced separation or joblessness, face a greater risk of separation and joblessness as adults. By age six, children in families who have experienced persistent intergenerational disadvantage have already fallen behind in academic performance and social-emotional development. Intergenerational disadvantage is pervasive and its effects upon the youngest generation of a family begin early.

Young people growing up in families with a history of intensive income-support are less likely to complete Year 12, are more likely to be in poor health, and have a higher prevalence of alcohol, tobacco and illicit drug use. Mental health also seems to be worse among the more disadvantaged. They are more likely to experience alcohol or drug abuse problems or trouble with the police. They are more likely to face unemployment, have children early, and receive income support (Pech, 2000, 13).

In 2009-10, of all couple families with resident dependent children, five per cent had neither parent employed. In 38 per cent of one-parent families with dependent children the resident parent was not employed. There were 667,000 dependent children (12 per cent) living in families without an employed resident parent. There were 568,000 dependent children (11 per cent) living in a household where no one was employed (ABS, 2011, 4). Long-term child poverty is strongly connected to the presence of only one parent in the household. Children living with only one parent have the highest permanent income poverty rates, while children living with both parents have the lowest permanent income poverty rates (Wilkins, 2014, 32).

Since 1980, single-parent families have accounted for at least half of all jobless families with children. Compared to working families, welfare dependent families are three and a half times as likely to have more than four children and three times as likely to have a youngest child under six years of age. The parents in income support dependent families are four times as likely to be unpartnered, and about twice as likely to have given birth before the age of twenty-one (Pech, 2000).

The big question is: how many children are born to a mother, while she is on a benefit? The Department of Social Services does not record the fact that a female may be pregnant while on income support. Rather, the Department records children who come into the care of income support recipients. The data, which the Department has kindly made available, relates to those children who either entitle their carers to a child-related income support payment or they are a dependent of an income support recipient. The principal carer is generally the person with the greater degree of care and control of the child. Only one person at a time can be assessed as the principal carer of a particular child. In some cases grandparents or other relatives or friends who have taken on responsibility of caring for the child can be determined to be the principal carer, where the person with legal responsibility is unable or unwilling to care for the child.

The Department has extracted records of all children born in the calendar year ending 2014 and merged the benefit history for major benefit types (females only) in the month prior to the birth and on the day of birth of the child. This merging method has produced two estimates of the potential number of children born to a woman while she was on a benefit. There were 58,829 children for major benefit types in the month prior to the birth. There were 63,950 children for major benefit types on the day of the birth of the child. Assuming these numbers occur every year, the number of children born to a mother while on a benefit in the course, for example, of a decade, could be as high as 600,000.

Australia, there is a problem

Evidence from studies on intergenerational welfare suggests that those on welfare are more likely than others to have trouble with authorities. The evidence does not prove that families receiving welfare are those same families whose children commit crimes, or are taken into care, or are abused. Nevertheless, there is abundant evidence of correlations between disadvantage and higher rates of substance abuse, domestic violence, child abuse, personal assault, and property crime (Bor, 2004; Cobb-Clark, 2009; Duncan, 2012; McLachlan, 2013; Shaw, 2006).

Evidence of causation would require knowledge of the welfare history of those who come before the courts. It is difficult to access such evidence. Nevertheless, there is sufficient available to indicate that those on welfare and from welfare families are far more likely than others to suffer the strife in families that leads to perhaps the most extreme government intervention in families: taking children from their parents.

In their hunger for headlines, news outlets that berate public officials for either taking children, or failing to take children, miss the point. Mistakes are made at the margin, but the need to remove children from parents is real, as the following case shows. The Melbourne case involved long-term permanent planning for five very young children aged between two and seven years. Child Protection workers discovered the four oldest children (one not yet having been born) alone at home, filthy and with scarcely anything to eat. It had been at least two days since they had seen their mother; their father had abandoned them some days earlier.

Once placed in care the children did not see their parents for some time. Eventually access was established but it was sporadic and it was clear that the parents were not in a position to resume care of the children. The children's paternal aunt rang Child Protection to offer to care for the children. She flew from Sydney and was quickly assessed as a suitable carer.

Although the foster care agency had been unable to place all four children together, Child Protection planned that aunty would take all four children at once. Given that she was living in a two bedroom flat and had other family obligations, it was not surprising that she said she was unable to take them at that time. All five children have been on Guardianship to Secretary Orders as their parents at that time had not been contactable. The children had never resided together since being placed in out-of-home care. The mother had agreed to have them placed permanently with carers. The children's father wished to have all five children placed in the care of his sister in Sydney.

The children were subject to profound neglect and traumatised by their exposure to violence. One of the children had recounted her memories of seeing her mother stabbing her father and 'Dad trying to break through the door and Daddy punching Mummy's teeth and punching [another child].' The father is not the biological father of the youngest child (Children's Court of Victoria, 2013).

There are some successes working with the most vulnerable families including those who have had children removed into care and those who have not (yet) had contact with the child protection system (Segal, 2011). But the intergenerational nature of the problem and its persistence suggests that new forms of intervention are required. Working people, by and large, wait until they can afford to have children. Some non-working people do not wait. The best way to have the non-working people mimic the working people is to have them practice reliable contraception. Withdrawal, condoms, even the pill are not wholly reliable. Abortions may work for some, but are not for all and, in any event, surely an ounce of prevention is worth a pound of cure. Family planning in Australia has a long and distinguished history. At special clinics and in many of the major public hospitals great efforts are made to inform men and women about fertility. Too many simply do not use these, often free, services. Others fail to heed advice.

Objections

The most common criticism of 'no contraception, no dole' has been that it is impractical. This is wrong. Right now almost every welfare beneficiary has to sit down with a public servant at Centrelink and talk about his or her obligation to the taxpayer for receipt of the benefit. The best time to intervene in a person's life, should intervention be warranted, is at the time they decide to take a welfare benefit. It is likely that they will be highly focused on talking to the person who holds the power over their income. At that time it can be made clear that, while on a benefit, they have an obligation not to conceive. The obligation would be easily satisfied by the recipient having a note from a (bulk-billing) doctor that they have entered on a course of long-acting reversible contraception (LARC). A doctor's note that it is not medically advisable would satisfy the obligation. A statement of conscientious objection would satisfy the obligation. Unfortunately, at present, LARCs are not available for men.

A minimum amount of support and a chance at life is an important feature of the Australian welfare state. It should remain so, but taxpayers decide who shall receive benefits and the circumstances under which they receive them. Where interference in individual liberty is modest and pay-off great, a level of compulsion is acceptable in Australian society. Some people's actions, in this case becoming pregnant, cause them to take benefits from others. If this action can be avoided at little or no detriment to the welfare beneficiary, and little or no detriment to the taxpayer, then the action may be warranted.

Australians accept many forms of government intervention in their lives, including taking children from incompetent parents. Counselling is compulsory before proceedings commence in the Family Court of Australia. Vaccination is compulsory for anyone on a benefit, including family payment. Hepatitis C is rife in the prison population. Research suggests that when a life-saving drug is available some prisoners do not comply. Only by having a nurse administer the drug each day is a cure successful. One source of the spread of Hepatitis C is thus eliminated. In the 1960s, seat belts became compulsory to install in cars and to wear when driving a motor vehicle (FORS, 1985). One source of death and injury from accidents was minimised.

The religious, Catholics especially, will argue the dignity of the individual and the sanctity of life would be violated under a no contraception, no dole regime. But Catholic women in England and the United States are as likely as any to take artificial contraception.[5]

---

5 Survey of 1,500 Catholics from parishes across England and Wales. Ruth Gledhill, 'Catholics ignore veto on the Pill.' *The Times* [London] 25 July 2008.

Evidence on contraceptive use from a nationally representative sample of women from the 2006-2008 National Survey of Family Growth (United States) showed that 98 per cent of sexually experienced Catholic women used a contraceptive method other than natural family planning. Further, 'only 2 per cent of Catholic women rely on natural family planning. Sixty-eight per cent of Catholic women use highly effective methods: sterilization, the pill or another hormonal method and the IUD' (Jones, 2011, 4).

A survey of Catholic students at a Catholic university in the United States concluded that 'the majority Catholic college students do not turn to the Church to influence their opinions on [contraception and pre-marital sex]; rather, they rely on their own lived experiences and the larger secular culture to inform them' (Maher, 2007, 85). Contraceptive use by Catholics is the norm, not the exception. Would Australian Catholic women differ in their attitudes to their English or American sisters?

Abortion is a more sensitive issue for Catholics than contraception, but even here the evidence is that Catholic practice is not so different from others. A study of 19,307 Australians aged 16-59 years compared members of four religious groups (Protestant, Catholic, Buddhist, Muslim) and two levels of frequency of attendance at religious service (less than monthly, at least monthly). Among women, only Catholics who attended church at least once a month were less likely than non-religious women to have had an abortion; Catholic women who attended church less than monthly were no less likely than non-religious women to have had an abortion (Visser, 2007, 44).

Catholic women who argue that 'an authentically pro-woman sexuality, a sexuality of equals, would advocate that women practice sexual restraint and demand men do the same' (Bachiochi, 2013, 162) may take heart from studies that suggest that early sex education about abstinence and birth control have been found to be 'associated with healthier sexual behaviour and outcomes' (Lindberg, 2012, 332). But the slogan coined by English suffragette Christabel Pankhurst, 'Votes for women and chastity for men', reminds women that the first was a breeze compared to the second. I would rather intervene to save women from irresponsible men than wait for men and women to give up on sex.

Some on the Left are outraged at the propsal because they believe that beneficiaries have rights. It is not a human right to raise a family at someone else's expense. Welfare rights are not human rights, they are gifts of other taxpayers, granted under very specific conditions. Those conditions may be changed, especially where there are benefits to the recipient and the taxpayer. The Left fret about overpopulation and climate change and are happy to argue for restricting childbirth in the name of saving the world from theoretical damage from climate change in 100 years. They appear not to worry, however, about the child to be born in nine months as a result of an unplanned, or an unsupported, pregnancy.

My libertarian colleagues may be squeamish about compulsory contraception for those who choose a benefit. They need to be reminded that it is not compulsory to take a benefit. Their hope, a world in which there are no benefits and charity alone steps in to help the unfortunate, is impractical. Stopping welfare may stop intergenerational welfare, but it would not stop intergenerational poverty. The welfare state is here to stay. I am a supporter, but it has a downside. It helps to create the next generation of dependent citizens. When someone chooses to take a benefit, it is reasonable for taxpayers to place conditions on the benefit. The condition lasts only so long as the person is on the benefit. If someone is on an unemployment benefit they should be searching for work, not starting a family. If someone is on a study benefit, they should be studying, not starting a family. If someone is on a parenting payment they should be bringing up their family, not adding to it. The disability pension is more problematic because it may be permanent. But, even in these cases, and depending on the circumstances, valid questions should be raised about having a child while on such a benefit.

Whether the policy, 'no contraception, no dole' should apply to every category of benefit will be a matter of judgment and depend, for example, on the number at risk in each class of benefit as a proportion of the number of beneficiaries.

2

An ounce of prevention is worth a pound of cure

What a LARC

According to an online survey by the Marie Stopes clinics, which provide pregnancy termination and other fertility services for women, although nearly 70 per cent of Australian women of reproductive age use a contraceptive method, approximately half will have 'an unplanned pregnancy' (Stopes, 2006, 4). A study of 3,434 women presenting for a termination of pregnancy in an Adelaide clinic between 1996 and 2006 found that 67 per cent of women used some form of contraception at the time of conception (Abigail, 2008, 235). These rates, similar to those in the United States (Finer, 2014, 43) may, in part, be explained by the fact that the combined oral contraceptive pill remains the preferred method of contraception in Australia as it is in the United States (Mazza, 2012).

Unplanned or unintended pregnancies encompass those pregnancies that occur earlier than desired as well as unwanted pregnancies, which is when no child, or no more children are desired. Each has consequences for the capacity of the mother and father to care for the child. An unwanted child may be loved and cared for, the same would hold for a child that arrived 'early', but with the unintended pregnancy comes the child for whom ideal provision – sufficient income and a stable relationship – has not been made. Perhaps something can be done to ensure that these pregnancies are intended.

A recent article in the *Medical Journal of Australia* argued that Australian women needed increased access to long-acting reversible methods of contraception (LARC) to reduce the number of unintended pregnancies and their associated costs. The LARC methods include 3-monthly progestogen injections, 3-year progestogen-only subdermal implants (rods), and 5- and 10-year intrauterine contraceptive methods. New Zealand suffers one of the highest rates of teenage pregnancy in the world, worse than Australia, although not as severe as the United States.[6] In July 2012 the New Zealand government commenced providing free LARCs to female welfare beneficiaries and their 16- to 19-year-old daughters.[7] The New Zealand government recognised the plight not only of the most vulnerable part of the population who experience unplanned pregnancy, teenage girls, but also the intergenerational nature of welfare dependence. Children of welfare dependent mothers and fathers are themselves more likely to become welfare dependent and more likely to suffer a range of social, health and economic problems (NZ MSD (a), 2012).

The Health Committee of the New Zealand House of Representatives in its inquiry on child abuse, unanimously and strongly supported the provision of LARCs free to welfare recipients (NZ HoR Health Committee, 2013, 15). The New Zealand public were very supportive. Nearly 80 per cent of respondents in a *Sunday Star-Times* reader poll and 65 per cent in a *Research New Zealand* poll supported funding LARCs for female beneficiaries. There were doubters. South Auckland Family Centre's Peter Sykes, for example, was reported as saying that his centre works with the same beneficiaries the scheme targets, but that many of them did not take advantage of available support because they were not 'engaged' with doctors or primary health providers.[8] In other words, beneficiaries were not taking advantage of services that were currently highly subsidised or free. The New Zealand government was right and brave to make LARCs freely available to a group most likely to benefit. The question for those who are not engaged, however, is what will it take to engage such people?

---

6 Statistics New Zealand, http://www.stats.govt.nz/browse_for_stats/population/births/teenage-fertility-in-nz.aspx accessed 26 February 2015.
7 Ministry of Social Development, New Zealand, http://www.msd.govt.nz/about-msd-and-our-work/newsroom/factsheets/budget/2012/contraception.html accessed 26 February 2015.
8 Nicola Russell, 'Free birth control wins public support.' 13 May 2012, http://www.stuff.co.nz/national/politics/6911369/Free-birth-control-wins-public-support accessed 26 February 2015.

Uptake of LARC methods in Australia is low. Only 6.5 per cent of women using contraception in Australia use LARC, in contrast to 15 per cent in northern Europe where, incidentally, teenage pregnancy rates (outside of the United Kingdom) are low (Black, 2013, 317). It appears that more Australian women need to be apprised of the facts that the typical male condom failure rate is approximately 18 per cent and oral contraceptive failure rate is nine per cent. LARC method failure rates rival that of tubal sterilisation, at less than one per cent (Stoddard, 2011, 970).

In her book about the recent emergence of women with life-long careers, Alison Wolf suggests that 'women can avoid an undesired pregnancy' (Wolf, 2013, 19). If only it were so. A recent sample of 1,000 sexually active women at Victorian clinics found 96 per cent of women reported use of some form of contraception. Of those, 89 per cent were confident in their knowledge of how to prevent pregnancy and 87 per cent stated it was important to avoid pregnancy at this stage in their life. It seems as though everything was under control. And yet, fully 37 per cent of the sample population were at risk of unintended pregnancy. They were at risk because eight per cent did not use any contraception (despite having said so in the initial survey), 31 per cent used an 'ineffective' contraception (withdrawal or rhythm method), and 61 per used contraception – condoms, oral contraceptive pills and withdrawal – inconsistently.

Some reasons why contraception fails

The two most common reasons for not using contraception consistently were, 'I did not have access to contraception when I needed it', and, 'I just forgot' (Ong, 2012, 3). Forgetting to use a contraception that requires daily vigilance or is spur-of-the-moment dependent is not a surprise. Couples are attracted to using withdrawal because 'it has no side effects, costs nothing, and does not require extra health care visits' (Ong, 2013, 74). The trouble is, it may fail.

The city of Kingston-upon-Hull in the north of England has

high levels of deprivation and social disadvantage, as well as high levels of teenage pregnancy and young motherhood. Compared to a pregnancy rate of 42 per 1,000 nationally, the rate amongst under-18 residents in Kingston-upon-Hull was 70 per 1,000. Of these, 37 per cent led to abortion. It appears that lack of knowledge about sex and contraception, and access to sexual health services, did not play a major role in unintended pregnancies among these young women. The decision making processes around choosing (or not) to use contraception were much more significant.

Young people do not use contraception consistently, and do not always think about it until after they become sexually active. Sex was often unplanned. This lack of planning lessened the likelihood of contraception being used, especially where alcohol was involved. One study in the city concluded, 'despite access to a range of contraception being relatively easy in theory, use of it depends more on the circumstances surrounding the sexual encounter. This is particularly the case when sex is unplanned or a 'one night stand' ' (Brown, 2010, 202).

A study of homeless youth and contraception use in the United States found that 'relationship commitment' emerged as the strongest correlate of not using effective contraceptives (Tucker, 2012, 258). Sex partners were important for emotional support, companionship, physical protection and material resources. One sentiment expressed was that having a child would be creating something positive, such as providing youth with someone to love, or creating or giving life to something. When asked why she would be pleased if she found out that she was pregnant, one 17-year-old answered:

> *If I had my own kid right now, it would give me something more to look forward to in life, because that would be my kid, and I would take care of him, and I could develop a good relationship with someone, finally. And if it's my kid, I'm going to make sure I take care of my kid better than my mom took care of me.*

In response to the same question, a 21-year-old male explained that a child is:

> *something that is going to love you back, and you can love it. [It's]*

something that I put in this world. It's like it's a gift.

A second positive theme was that having a child would improve respondents' intimate relationships. For example, when asked what 'one of the best things about being a mom would be', one 18-year-old answered:

> *It could bring me and my boyfriend closer … He's been wanting a kid with me. … he really wants a baby, and he wants me to be the mother.*

Some have suggested that disadvantaged youth may want to get pregnant because they lack realistic paths to achieve traditional middle-class markers of adulthood, such as graduation and full-time employment, and they view parenthood as an achievable and desirable path to of adult status (Tucker, 2012, 259). There is some back-to-front thinking going on among some young people. That some want a child or believe that having one may make them more grown up is not really a reason to support an essentially immature decision.

A study of Irish men and women aged 18-45 years on the use of contraception in 2003 concluded that the consistency of contraceptive use was higher among women than men with lower use in unskilled manual social classes for both sexes. 'Not having planned for sex' was the most commonly cited reason for non-use (47 per cent of men and 40 per cent of women). 'Not caring if pregnancy occurred' was cited by 11 per cent of women and 12 per cent of men, while 'took a chance' was cited by eight per cent of both men and women. Semi and unskilled manual women were more likely to report that sex was unplanned or that they 'took a chance' (Layte, 2007, 477).

Those most likely

The evidence for those most likely to have an unintended pregnancy is readily identifiable. Four recent Australian studies provide a solid profile:

1. A study of nearly 400,000 consultations across Australia between GPs and females of reproductive age on the

management of contraception undertaken between 2007 and 2011 concluded that female patients who were indigenous, spoke a language other than English at home or held a Commonwealth Health Care Card had significantly lower general contraceptive management rates (Mazza, 2012, 111).

2. A study of 1,006 women attending three Family Planning Victoria clinics in 2011 found that having more than one partner in the last three months was associated with higher failures to avoid unintended pregnancies. Having the same partner for longer periods of time was shown to be associated with consistent contraceptive use. The nature of the relationship also seemed to correlate with likelihood of using contraception. For instance, if a woman was in a more romantic, caring close relationship, the couple had a higher likelihood of using contraception than those in casual and uncommitted relationships (Ong, 2012, 9).

3. A study of 1,554 women presenting for antenatal care to a large metropolitan hospital in Sydney from 2010 to 2011 found that 68 per cent of pregnancies were clearly intended, 30 per cent were ambivalent and more than two per cent experienced an unplanned pregnancy. Those more likely to experience an unintended pregnancy were women under 25 years old, unmarried women and women of Asian background. The findings were used to argue that 'an effective strategy to address unintended pregnancy is to improve access to long-acting reversible contraceptives' (Rassi, 2013, 572).

4. Somewhat surprisingly, religion does not play a large part in preventing sexual activity and, by implication, the risk of pregnancy, especially among young women. A study of 1,324 young women living in New South Wales or the Australian Capital Territory in 1998, and had given birth

in the year preceding, or who had terminated a pregnancy, concluded that religious affiliation does not appear to delay sexual experience. Respondents who reported having no religion initiated sexual intercourse earliest, followed by those of Christian religion.

Being a regular church-goer was associated with a slightly higher mean age at first sexual intercourse, with little difference between those who attended church occasionally or never. The difference in age of first sexual intercourse for Catholic girls and girls of no religion was 15 years and 4 months versus 14 years and 9 months. The age of Muslim girls at first intercourse was 17 years and 6 months. Those whose parents were married at the time of the girl's first encounter was 15 years and 5 months, for those who parents never lived together was 14 years and 4 months (Evans, 2000, 148).

Family planning and sex education aplenty

Some characteristics of women most likely to remain at greatest risk of unintended pregnancy is known and the reasons why are mostly understood. At the same time, efforts to intervene to assist them in their choices are also well explored.

A recent investigation of the relationship between school-based sex education policies and sexual health-related statistics of young people in Australia, and elsewhere, concluded that although no single factor was entirely responsible for sexual health outcomes such as unwanted pregnancy rates, comprehensive sex education appears to be one of the more effective means 'of empowering youth against the negative consequences of sexual activity' (Weaver, 2005, 184). For example, in NSW schools, sex, gender and reproduction are first discussed in the syllabus in years five and six to schoolchildren aged between 10 and 12 years (Mistler, 2008, 444). This is not to argue that more could not be achieved in sex education by introducing the subject at an earlier age (Walsh, 2013, 37), or that sub-groups whose school attendance is poor miss out (Mistler, 2008, 446). Judging from the literature, however, there appears to be a crowded agenda with discussion about the poor results of the 'abstinence' approach to sex education and a greater emphasis on sexuality education to account for the needs of homosexuals. For all of this education, unintended pregnancy is high. Lack of knowledge about sex does not appear to be the problem.

Added to school-based sex education is the tradition of family planning in Australia, which has a long and distinguished pedigree. There are no longer backroom abortion clinics of last century, or male doctors with attitudes of last century. There are a very large number of government and non-government providers in Australia that look after the full gamut of reproductive and sexual health of women and men.

Sexual Health and Family Planning Australia (SHFPA), for example, is the national peak body for the six state and two territory sexual health and family planning organisations. Collectively, they provide a range of sexual and reproductive health clinical services, community education, professional training and research. In 2011, SHFPA provided over a quarter of a million clinical services to the public. This included cancer prevention through pap smears and vaccinations, contraception and family planning services, and sexually transmitted infection (STI) diagnosis and treatment. It included provision of specialist sexual and reproductive health workforce training and development including GPs, nurses and Aboriginal health workers. It also included education and health promotion to primary and secondary school teachers, students, community workers, government agencies, disability workers and the general public.[9]

In October 2014 SHFPA issued a statement supporting increasing the use of LARC methods in Australia.[10] It called for a policy whereby all women seeking contraception should be given accurate

9 Sexual Health and Family Planning Australia, http://www.shfpa.org.au/sites/shfpa. drupalgardens.com/files/201310/LARCstatementSHFPAFINAL.pdf   accessed   28 February 2015.
10 Family Planning NSW, http://www.fpnsw.org.au accessed 28 February 2015.

evidence-based information on the safety, efficacy, advantages and disadvantages of all methods and assisted to make a choice based on their personal needs, preferences and medical suitability. In addition to SHFPA, government and community controlled, but usually government-funded, sexual health clinics are very widespread in Australia.[11] Family Planning NSW, for example, has five fixed clinics in NSW (Ashfield, Fairfield, Penrith, Newcastle and Dubbo) and provides services in locations throughout the state with more 28,000 client visits annually.[12]

Family Planning Queensland makes the obvious point that family planning advice and counselling services can be accessed through a local General Practitioner, in addition to Family Planning Queensland services, which are located in nine cities in Queensland.[13] There are also 28 indigenous health centres located throughout Queensland.[14] Children-by-Choice is a pro-choice women-centered organisation in Queensland, which provides unplanned pregnancy information on all options: abortion, adoption and parenting. Its banner boasts, '40 years 200,000 women.'[15] Marie Stopes International Australia centres, known as 'Dr Marie' centres, offer a full range of sexual and reproductive health care, including pregnancy counselling, medical and surgical abortion, contraception, STI testing and treatment, cervical screening and vasectomy through 15 centres Australia-wide.[16] It is possible for women and men in Australia to make contact with a knowledgeable person to assist them with an unintended pregnancy. It is unlikely that access to services is the stopper to better prevention, but ignorance, attitudes and poor incentives may be.

---

11 Queensland Government, Queensland Health, http://www.health.qld.gov.au/clinical-practice/guidelines-procedures/sex-health/services/default.asp#qld accessed 28 February 2015.

12 Family Planning NSW, http://www.fpnsw.org.au accessed 28 February 2015.

13 Queensland Government, http://www.qld.gov.au/health/children/pregnancy/unplanned/index.html accessed 3 March 2015.

14 Queensland Aboriginal and Islander Health Council, http://www.qaihc.com.au/members/ accessed 3 March 2015.

15 Children by Choice, http://www.childrenbychoice.org.au/if-youre-pregnant/im-considering-an-abortion/clinics-interstate accessed 28 February 2015.

16 Marie Stopes International Australia, http://www.mariestopes.org.au/where-we-work/australia/ accessed 28 February 2015.

What about men?

Forming multiple relationships and having children in those relationships is a recurring theme in this area. Take a case in the Family Court of Australia of competing applications from mother and father for parenting of a five-year-old child. The Secretary of the NSW Department of Family and Community Services intervened in the matter. The parents formed a relationship in 2008 when the mother was 19 and the father 30. The child was born the following year. Although together only intermittently, they maintained a relationship until 2010 when they separated. Post-separation the child, by consent, lived with the father and spent time with the mother.

The mother has a new partner. Mr A. She has a daughter from that relationship, G, aged one. She is hoping to be able to live with Mr A full-time if court orders permit. In mid-2010 the father formed a new relationship with Ms P and lived with her for two years. Ms P was pregnant (with H) to another man when the relationship began. She also had three young children from her prior marriage to Mr K.

The father has a son, M, from a prior relationship with Ms P. M was also a member of the household. In 2012, Mr K raised allegations about sexual misconduct by M with one of the children of Ms P, allegations substantiated by the Joint Investigation Response Team. The K family children were moved to live with their father. In mid-2012 the father and Ms P reluctantly ended their relationship. The K family children returned to live with Ms P.

The father has had relationships with more than one woman who has been the victim of domestic violence – women with chaotic family lives. The mother has had relationships with at least two men who have been violent towards her and a risk to children. The judge considered that 'both parents need to be especially careful of future relationships' (Family Court of Australia (b), 2014).

It would be a good thing if, in addition to being especially careful of relationships, men were ready or able to control their fertility. The promise of safe and reliable LARCs for men has been long awaited, but the messages from the scientific community are mixed.

Among the approaches undertaken for the development of new male contraceptives, hormonal methods are potentially closest to a possible clinical application. Availability of male hormonal contraceptives could provide the male partner with an opportunity to share the family planning responsibility, and give men in general the opportunity to gain control over their fertility.

Despite significant progress showing the contraceptive efficacy of hormonal regimens for men, in comparison to female hormonal methods and their feasibility and acceptability, research in this field has not yet led to an approved product. Some suggest that the promise of new contraceptive drugs is real. With the best combinations, about 95 per cent of men can have optimal contraceptive protection, similar to the female hormonal contraceptives. Others suggest that development of a marketable hormonal product for male contraception remains an unreachable goal. Apparently, no major drug company has shown interest in leading this project to a market that does not seem profitable or free from possible litigation. So far, no concerted action between the scientific community and governments has been undertaken to change this situation (Liu, 2006; Meriggiola, 2014).

An alternative but still experimental solution is reversible sterility using injectable polymer RISUG. Experiments during the last two decades using RISUG promises to sterile men for a period of up to 15 years. According to recent studies in animal models, it proves to be completely reversible. Practically, there are no better options available that can assure complete sterility and precise reversibility. Unfortunately, advancement of this injectable polymer is slow, and the clinical trials are not providing robust conclusions. It is, however, understandable that treatment with RISUG and its follow up in human subjects is a difficult task. Subjects normally do not want to talk about it after injection unless there are any complications, and the follow-up must be done for a long time to report polymer's efficacy and side effects. After reversal the patients are difficult to track (Lohiya, 2014, 70).

For the foreseeable future men will not take a direct interest in contraception any more than they do now. Vasectomy works for those who have completed a family, so they are not of much help in the task of lifting the burden from those most likely to experience unintended pregnancy.

Ethics

It would be unconscionable to leave a person, man, woman or child, without income support. The point of the welfare system is to avoid such a situation. Moreover, it could be argued that it is not ethical, in effect, to pay women to have children whom they cannot support. Alternative proposals should not, therefore, be assessed as if present policies were ethical. Alternative proposals should be as ethical as the present, but need be no more so. Take, as an example, Project Prevention in the United States. It offers $US300 to addicted individuals who agree either to undergo surgical sterilisation or use LARCs. Project Prevention boasts that it has 'paid addicts in 50 states and the District of Columbia.'[17] Paying people to use LARCS is a halfway house between the New Zealand model of providing LARCs free to beneficiaries and the present proposal, which is making LARCs a condition of benefit.

A recent discussion considered whether financial incentives are acceptable motivators for changing health behaviour, particularly in family planning decisions and, if so, whether it is possible to develop ethically acceptable guidelines to encourage addicted women to use LARCs (Lucke, 2012, 1039). Women with substance abuse issues report difficulties using conventional systems of care for a number of reasons, including a mistrust of health-care services, fear of forced treatment or fear of losing custody of children, guilt, denial or embarrassment regarding their substance use, stigma and the costs and difficulty of accessing services. These women face other barriers in accessing contraception including a belief that contraception is not needed due to impaired fertility while in drug treatment (e.g. methadone) and misinformation about different methods.

---

17 Project Prevention (US), http://www.projectprevention.org accessed 4 March 2015.

Financial incentives are being used to motivate people to quit smoking, manage chronic health better, lose weight and eat more healthily. Vouchers, which can be exchanged for goods and services, are being offered to addicts provided they submit to proof of abstinence. Incentives have been used in developing countries where clients have been provided with vouchers to purchase family planning advice, prevention and management of STIs, care for sexual assault and safe abortions. Incentives are designed to capitalise on a tendency for most people to prefer smaller, more immediate rewards to larger rewards that occur later in time. Personal payments appear to be more effective than information, or free services, in changing behaviour and they are less restrictive than legislation that compels change or punishes people for failing to act in a healthy way. Then again, taxation on cigarettes seems to have caused a decline in smoking rates, particularly in stymying the uptake among the young.

The fear is that a too generous incentive distorts judgement by encouraging people to underestimate the risks and overestimate the benefits of participation. Large payments are problematic if they compromise the validity of a woman's consent. Apparently, incentives for reproductive health promotion in other settings have typically been much more modest. For example, a pilot program in Australia offers $AUD10 for young people to undergo STI testing. Large cash payments could exacerbate harms by enabling addicts to purchase larger than usual quantities of drugs. On the other hand, non-addicted participants may use a cash incentive for harmful purposes. Empirical studies have found that incentives of $70 and $100 in cash are not associated with increased drug use. Participants who received cash payments were also more likely to attend follow-up appointments than those who received gift vouchers. Payment in the form of vouchers or goods and services (e.g. food, clothing, health care) may be less likely to exacerbate harm immediately, but they may be worth less than cash and thus be less attractive.

An addicted person's decision-making capacity would be impaired if they were intoxicated and in acute withdrawal, but this would not necessarily be true of addicted people who are not in either of these states. It could be argued that there are circumstances in which an addicted woman could give informed consent to contraceptive choices when offered financial incentives to do so. These could include, for example: only seeking consent for the procedure after a clinical consultation with an independent health-care provider; giving addicted women time to reflect on their choice; not offering a financial incentive that is large or immediate; offering reversible forms of long-acting contraception instead of surgical procedures; and providing addicted women with adequate independent information about their contraception options. These approaches would respect the autonomy of addicted women while increasing their access to methods of contraception.

A response to incentives and compulsion is that they undermine the need to 'address systemically the barriers to reproductive health in this population, somehow presupposing that this group of women are incapable of informed decision-making.' Such responses hope upon hope that more 'consumer information' and 'accessible health care' will solve all the problems (Black, 2012, 1362). Decades of good information and free and highly subsidised services may not have reduced intergenerational welfare to a level that could be achieved. Indeed, they may have induced them. No advocate of incentives is suggesting denying access to good advice. Setting up more and more clinics, more outreach, and more jobs for the caring profession will not solve the fact that many do not take advantage of good advice, or that there are enduring and seemingly irremovable barriers to the goal of planned pregnancy. There is a calculus to be made about the gain and pain to individuals of any proposal, as it has to be made for others involved, in particular, taxpayers who support benefits.

Constrained choice is not compulsion

In the best of worlds no child should be born unwanted or to a parent, or parents, unable or unwilling to care for them. While conditional benefits and incentives to use LARCs have a part to play, there are cases where the state must intervene to stop a pregnancy. In 2015, a judge of the United Kingdom Court of Protection declared that a woman, identified only as DD, lacked capacity to litigate and to make decisions in respect of contraception. The judge decided that it was in DD's best interests to undergo a therapeutic sterilisation. He ordered authorities 'to remove DD from her home and take steps to convey her to hospital for the purposes of the sterilisation procedure, and authorise the use of reasonable and proportionate measures to ensure that she is able to receive the said treatment even if any deprivation of liberty is caused by the same' (Court of Protection, 2015, 140). This was a deeply shocking and troubling case. But the judge was right to make the order.

DD was a 36-year old woman with Autistic Spectrum Disorder and mild to borderline learning disability with a full scale IQ of 70. She displayed characteristics consistent with an attachment disorder, likely to have resulted from her experience of physical and possibly sexual abuse as a child or young person. As an adult, DD had an extraordinary, tragic, and complex obstetric history. At the time of the case, she had had six children aged between six months and 12 years, all of whom were being raised by permanent substitute carers, five of them in adoptive homes. DD had had no continuing contact with any of her children. DD had never demonstrated the desire or capacity to engage with the level of support, which was likely to be required to assure a child's safety in her care. DD was in a long-term relationship, which included a sexual relationship, with BC. BC had a significant learning disability, with a full scale IQ in the region of 62, and displayed some traits of an Autistic Spectrum Disorder.

The judge stressed that the case [was] not about eugenics. Rather, the 'outcome has been driven by the bleak yet undisputed evidence that a further pregnancy would be a significantly life-threatening event for DD.' The Applicants' obstetric, gynaecological and contraceptive experts strongly recommended the treatment for DD: 'The risk to [DD] of a future pregnancy, especially if concealed, is highly likely to lead to her death' (Court of Protection, 2015, 8). Not exactly a brave call. What about the six children before that, each one taken from the mother and placed in care? Surely, at least in these cases, while in receipt of a benefit, a woman must be placed on contraception.

A precedent of sorts is found in a recent decision of the Victorian Civil and Administrative Tribunal. A 46 year-old woman on a disability pension, was refused access to assisted reproductive treatment because, at various times, orders had been made removing four children from the applicant's custody or guardianship. The applicant was a mother to seven children to three fathers. The application for assisted reproduction was with her partner who was on a service pension. The tribunal decided against permitting access on the grounds that 'the paramount consideration is the best interests of a child to be born' (Victorian CAT, 2015, 171). It is worth exploring such cases and, as well, less extreme cases where it is likely that children will end up in care and to which an ounce of prevention is worth a pound of cure.

Conclusion

The point of the 'no contraception, no dole' policy is to take the opportunity for women to control their fertility, at little or no cost and minimal inconvenience and risk, in order to improve their chances of caring for those children they have or wish to have. It is not a case of brute force and compulsion. There are lessons to learn from both the incentive schemes in the United States and elsewhere, and the free schemes in New Zealand. Free may be ineffective. Incentives may be more effective but carry some unintended consequences. Both are worthy avenues to pursue, but compulsion as an obligation of receipt of benefit may be best. It should be made clear, a teenage mother who is not on a benefit would not be subject to the compulsory LARC policy. To make LARCs compulsory because, for example, parents of teenage girls were on a benefit would be a step too far. Nevertheless, where a mother is subject to the policy, the New Zealand option of making LARCs available free to a teenage daughter would be worth exploring.

'No contraception, no dole' takes a woman at the point when she will be willing to listen: she will be asking for taxpayer support. The taxpayer should talk to her, through the delegate of the Department of Social Services and professionals in the health field, to ensure that the best available LARC is available while she remains on the benefit. Benefits are not forever, so protection need only last as long as the benefit. Once the person is re-established, they will be in a stronger position than may otherwise have been the case to start life again, and a family if that is their wish.

3

Intergenerational welfare

Intergenerational welfare – not working for some recipients

Intergenerational welfare occurs when a welfare recipient is the son or daughter of a welfare recipient. The likelihood of children being on welfare as adults increases if parents have been on welfare. It does not follow that 'welfare' is to blame for intergenerational dependence and that welfare should be withdrawn. Neither does it follow that the recipient is to blame, nor necessarily that they should in some way be made to account for their circumstances. Bad things happen to people, things that make it difficult to survive. Having insurance to protect against the bad times is a very good idea so long as the benefits do not induce bad habits or poor choices. The extent to which families make poor choices or pass on bad traits and habits the costs of which are a burden to others, the so-called 'fiscal externalities of parenthood', is at the heart of intergenerational welfare dependence (Folbre, 2012, 39).

Adverse events yes, bad choices and behaviour no

Life is not always kind, major adverse events, such as illness and injury, come along and cause overwhelming hardship. The figures in table 3.1 show the average annual prevalence of adverse events among Australians. Of course, many positive events occur as well, such as births, marriages, promotions and not all adverse events force someone onto a benefit, or onto a benefit for long. Nevertheless, the need for a welfare system is apparent.

Table 3.1. Average annual prevalence of adverse life events, 2002-11 (per cent)

Separated from spouse or long-term partner	3.5
Serious personal injury or illness to self	7.5
Serious injury or illness to a close relative or family member	14.0
Death of spouse or child	1.0
Victim of physical violence	1.5
Detained in jail, or close family member detained in jail	2.0
Dismissed from job	2.5

Source: (Wilkins, 2014, 18)

The time that Australians remain on a benefit depends on their situation. Figure 3.1 shows the numbers of recipients and duration on selected benefits.[18] The payments range from student payments (Austudy) that need relatively short term assistance to support their studies, to longer periods for single mothers and fathers (parenting payments) while they have young children, to lengthy periods for the disabled (disability support pension). Within these payments there is considerable variation. Some of the unemployed require newstart allowance for less than a year, but many require it for five to 10 years. Many disabled require the DSP for less than a year, but most require it for more than 10 years. They may thereafter move to the age pension (which is not featured in the table).

---

18 Family benefits and childcare subsidies are counted as income support in the social security system and the age pension is excluded.

Figure 3.1. Number of recipients for selected payments by duration, 2014

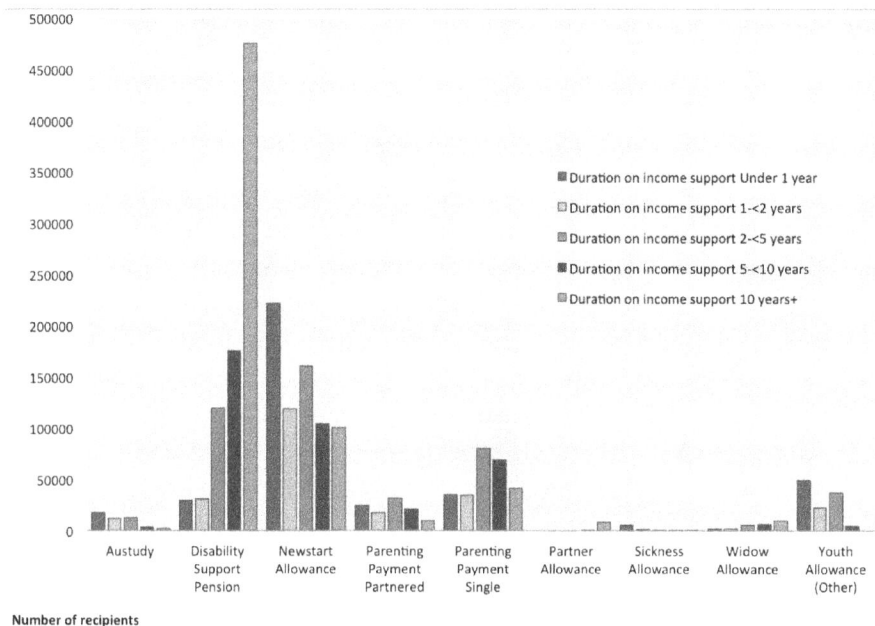

500000
450000
400000
350000
300000
250000
200000
150000
100000
50000
0

■ Duration on income support Under 1 year
□ Duration on income support 1-<2 years
■ Duration on income support 2-<5 years
■ Duration on income support 5-<10 years
▨ Duration on income support 10 years+

Austudy | Disability Support Pension | Newstart Allowance | Parenting Payment Partnered | Parenting Payment Single | Partner Allowance | Sickness Allowance | Widow Allowance | Youth Allowance (Other)

Number of recipients

Source: Department of Social Security, 'Duration of income support.' (Excel) June 2014

The obligations that attend each benefit vary. The circumstances that lead to the need for access to the age and disability pension are not controllable by the recipient and so obligations are few. Access to a study benefit, however, is a choice and an investment in the future, in the anticipation of a return through better skills. Receipt of Austudy carries an obligation to succeed in education or training. Unemployment (and temporary and lesser disability) benefit carries obligations to be available for work.

Benefits must never serve as an inducement to not work, which is why, for example, there are considerable obligations attached to receipt of newstart allowance. Parenthood, especially single parenthood, is fraught, so parenting payments have few obligations. Support for people to become parents can be anticipated and controlled however. Becoming a parent while on a benefit should not occur because, depending on the recipient, it may well cause intergenerational dependence.

Are the losers of today, losers for life?

Losers of today do not need to be losers for life, but to increase the chance that they are not requires knowing something about them. Australian research on the extent to which income support receipt by young people is associated with their parents' previous income support is quite recent. The Family and Community Services Transgenerational Data Set (1996) contains selected information from Family Allowance and income support records of some 53,000 young people and their 92,000 parents. This is an extraordinarily powerful data set.

Research based on the data compared different families, which ranged from those who had received Family Allowance for the young person at some time but were no longer doing so, effectively a non-recipient group, to long-term social security recipient families, with both parents or the lone parent on a social security pension or benefit.

The results from this study (and supplemented by others) were stark. Early motherhood was twice as likely in long-term social security recipient families as non-recipient families. Being a lone-parent family was almost three times as likely in long-term social security recipient families. Young mothers were more likely not to have a partner in long-term social security recipient families. Having more than four children was three and a half times as likely in long-term social security recipient families. Having a youngest child less than six years of age was three times as likely in long-term social security recipient families (Pech, 2000, 48).

Young people were five times more likely to be receiving income support, including unemployment benefit, in long-term social security recipient families. Young people were about two-thirds as likely again to receive a disability payment in long-term income support recipient families.[19] Evidence from the Youth in Focus Project, a major and more recent longitudinal Australian study, suggested behavioural and other problems as well. Problems such as being suspended from, expelled from, or chronically late to school, less likely to be studying, suffering poorer health including mental health, and more likely to experience higher prevalence of alcohol, tobacco and illicit drug use (Cobb-Clark & Sartbayeva, 2010; Cobb-Clark, 2010).

Young beneficiaries were also more likely to come from troubled families. The likelihood of a young person experiencing high levels of income support dependence was more than twice others if they come from an income support recipient family, almost twice as likely if they lived with only one parent, and three and a half times as likely if they had a primary indigenous parent. The primary parents in long-term social security recipient families were four times as likely to be unpartnered, two and a half times as likely to have been born overseas, eight times as likely to identify as indigenous, and about twice as likely to have given birth before the age of twenty-one. They were 25 times as likely to be living in public housing.

To the difficulties of indigenous families can be added those that sometimes arise with a non-indigenous partner. An example is featured in a recent court case of a parenting dispute over the child of an indigenous mother and white father, where the paternal grandmother cared for the child.

The child was born of a one-year relationship between her mother and father. The father was born and had grown up in the Latrobe Valley area of Victoria. The mother was an Aboriginal woman of the West Arrernte culture, and had grown up in her community in Central Australia. The mother and father met and commenced a relationship in 2003, when the mother was living in the South Australian community of Ernabella, and the father had travelled from Victoria to Ernabella to work at the local carnival. The mother had two children from a previous relationship with a white Anglo-Australian, who was working with the carnival when it had previously visited the Ernabella

---

19 In some cases the parent's long-term income support receipt may have arisen from the need to care for the young person.

community. Those children each speak, to varying degrees, English, Pitjantjara, Arrernte and Luritja.

After a period of traveling through Central Australia, the mother and father returned to the Latrobe Valley. They separated in 2004, about one month before the child was born. When the child was aged approximately seven days, the mother left the Latrobe Valley for Central Australia, 'in order to attend to indigenous women's business'.

The mother's income was derived from Centrelink and included a parenting payment with family tax allowances. For the past 10 years, she had lived in and out of the Ernabella community, which is located in the northern region of South Australia, and approximately 800 km north of Adelaide. The mother's case was that the child should live with her 'to be raised within Aboriginal culture and kinship' whereby the child would travel to, live in and be educated in other Aboriginal communities within Central Australia. Extended family and elders would assist in her physical, cultural and emotional upbringing (Family Court of Australia, 2007).

From another Australian source, the Longitudinal Study of Australian Children, families that were ever lone-parent families were substantially more likely where either set of the study child's grandparents had separated. The chances were higher still if both the maternal and paternal grandparents had separated. Similarly, the proportion of parents who were jobless was much higher where either or both the maternal and paternal grandparents had also experienced family joblessness, compared to families where neither set of grandparents had this experience (Hancock, 2012, 55).

A recent court case, which concerned parenting orders for the care of six Aboriginal children aged between 11 years and four years is a good illustration of the intergenenertional problems suffered by some families. The applicant was the maternal grandmother.

As a result of the children's neglect and regular exposure to drugs, alcohol and violence in their parents' household, the grandmother took the children to live with her in Redfern. The six children remained in the grandmother's care in her small two-bedroom Redfern home. She then took them to live at the home of the grandmother's former partner and father/step father to her children.

In 2014, the Department of Family and Community Services removed the six children from the grandmother's care. The maternal grandmother 'is exposing the children to persons who use alcohol; exposing the children to verbal violence.' The maternal grandmother, aged 45 years, had recently moved and lived with two of her daughter's children (the subject of these proceedings), and her youngest daughter (aged 16 years) who was under the care of the Minister. She had three other daughters; another daughter died in 2010. Ms K was the mother of the children. Ms A (another of the grandmother's daughters) was the mother of three children who have been the subject of intervention by the Department. Ms A and Ms D (another of the grandmother's daughters) had each given birth to another child in the last year.

The grandmother was in a long-term relationship with Mr W until 2012. Thereafter the grandmother was in a relationship with an Aboriginal man, and had the care of his two children, aged three and five years. She was supported by a disability support pension and a family tax benefit. The mother was unemployed. She continued to abuse alcohol and illicit drugs, mainly cannabis and occasional 'ice'. She smoked marijuana every night. The father was living with his step-brother's family. He was one of nine children all removed from their parents' care by the Department. He was placed from the age of eight years in up to 15 different foster homes. He started using cannabis at the age of 12 years. The father was unemployed (Federal Circuit Court of Australia, 2014).

Young parents are not all 'teenage mothers' and, in any event, the percentage of teenage mothers in Australia has declined in recent decades (ABS (a), 2015, 8), but the circumstances of teenage mothers are less favourable than those of older mothers.[20] Compared to older mothers, teenage mothers have relatively disadvantaged

20 Based on data from the Department of Families, Housing, Community Services and Indigenous Affairs' Household, Income and Labour Dynamics in Australia survey.

childhood, are less likely to be partnered or be married at the time
the first child was born, and are more likely to be unemployed, as
are the teenage mothers' partners. Teenage mothers are much more
likely to rely on welfare throughout their lifetimes, are more likely to
suffer poor health and to receive disability support pension (Jeon,
2011, 246).

The age of teenage mothers is not necessarily the cause of the
difficulties of their offspring. The findings from a study of teenage
mothers and their offspring (at age 14) who received antenatal care in
Brisbane showed that the 14 year-old offspring of mothers who were
aged 18 years and younger compared to those who were offspring
of older mothers were more likely to have disturbed psychological
behaviour, poorer school performance, poorer reading ability. They
were more likely to have been in contact with the criminal justice system
and were more likely to smoke regularly and to consume alcohol. The
associations between maternal age and psychological distress, school
performance, and smoking and alcohol use were, however, largely
explained by socioeconomic factors, maternal depression, family
structure and maternal smoking (Shaw, 2006, 2526).

Intergenerational bad habits

There are strong suggestions that those on welfare come from troubled
families, and that members of troubled families behave poorly. Those
habits are passed on, generation after generation. Young Australians
growing up in disadvantaged households, for example, are more likely to
take a number of health risks such as smoking, drinking, illicit drug use,
and take social risks such as running away from home, or behaviours
that would have them come into contact with police and the courts.
They are also more likely to have health problems such as asthma
and depression as they enter adulthood. Most of the risky behaviour
is explained by family structure, in particular the mothers' own risk-
taking behaviour (in particular smoking) and the level of 'investment' in
children's education, specifically, reading to them at night.

A recent court case illustrates the problem of a combination of issues. The case concerned a 12-year-old child currently in foster care and whether the child should be reunited with the mother. A protection order was sought because the mother had resumed heroin use. The child said of the mother: 'She said that she was miserable because her mother was a junkie spending all the food money on drugs.'

The mother's two previous partners were heroin users: 'The mother has been very controlled and/or very influenced by those two ex-partners. There was a time in the father's life when he was a heroin user. As far as ever happens with a heroin user that appears to be in the past.' The father is still a user of cannabis. The father is bipolar. 'The mother has not yet progressed sufficiently with drug treatment and has not yet provided sufficient clean urine screens for me to be satisfied that her risk of relapse is an acceptable risk. In those circumstances I consider that it would place the child at unacceptable risk of emotional harm to be returned at present to her mother' (Children's Court of Victoria (c), 2009).

Problems of welfare dependence may extend to poor dietary habits. The Growing Up in Australia: The Longitudinal Study of Australian Children (LSAC) studies tracked eating habits of Australian children. The results were unsurprising. Children, whose parents exercised, did not smoke or binge drink, ate more fruit and vegetables and less energy-dense (junk) foods. Children of mothers with poor habits ate less fruit and vegetable. Unhealthy eating habits in children, which are likely maintained through to adolescence and adulthood, were more likely to be male, from low income families, single-parent families, rural areas, have parents with no university degree, were not breastfed at six months of age, and have mothers with less healthy eating and lifestyle practices (ABS, 2003; Daraganova, 2013).

The LSAC also examined the differences in children's activity levels, dietary intake and Body Mass Index according to parental status to determine the likelihood of childhood overweight and obesity in a single-parent household. There were higher rates of overweight and obesity in girls aged four to nine whose parents were single. Children in single-parent households watched more television, ate more food high in fat and sugar and less fresh fruit and vegetables than children from dual-parent households. The findings suggested that an additive effect of dietary and activity variables may contribute to the higher rates of overweight and obesity in Australian children, and that girls from single-parent households may be particularly at risk (Byrne, 2011, 415).

Anti-social behaviour and crime

A study based on the Mater University Study of Pregnancy, an ongoing longitudinal investigation of women's and children's health and development involving over 8,000 participants identified a range of significant risk factors for early adolescent anti-social behaviour. Children whose mothers experienced more than one marital change were at increased risk and others have noted the importance of marital disruption in leading to adolescent involvement in crime. The findings indicated that poor language ability increases the risk of anti-social behaviour (Bor, 2004, 370).

In a recent court case, a child's maternal grandmother brought an application for sole parental responsibility. The child had been living mostly with the maternal grandmother for more than five years, in both New Zealand and Australia. The maternal grandmother's household consisted of herself, the child and also the maternal great-grandmother. The mother lived alone in a suburb of Sydney. She was expecting another child. In relation to the child she was expecting, the mother said she was not living with the child's father and was not 'too sure' as to whether the relationship would be ongoing. She anticipated moving to a bigger house but was not 'too sure'. She did not presently hold a driver's licence due to unpaid fines. She did not have a car.

The maternal grandmother remarried four years after the birth of the mother. The mother was raised by her mother and step-father, who had recently separated. There was evidence of a violent relationship for the maternal grandparents. The mother appeared before a court in New Zealand for various offences, which could generally be described as anti-social. The mother's relationship with the father was a violent and volatile one. Each was involved in violent conduct and both parties were found with cannabis and stolen goods.

Soon after the birth of the child there was a violent incident in which the father assaulted the mother. The mother came to the attention of police through buying equipment that could be used for making drugs. The mother had a history of unstable relationships. She had intense feelings of anger and rejection and her identity was poorly developed. The judge noted impulsive and violent acts such as attacking a taxi driver and allowing the man with a gun into her house (Family Court of Australia (b), 2015).

A 2010 study of six extended families in Tasmania, with an offending history spanning several generations, and involving 714 family members, found that the more serious the parent's criminal record, the greater the probability of their children subsequently committing offences, with the influence of the father's record seemingly being greater than that of the mother. Where neither parent had a criminal record, there was a 76 per cent probability their male offspring would have no criminal record, although there was a 19 per cent probability their male offspring would have a criminal record for serious criminal offences. However, where the son had a father with a criminal record but a mother with no record, the probability of the son having a criminal record for serious offences increased by almost 30 percentage points. By contrast, where a son had a father without a criminal record but a mother who had committed crimes, the probability of the son having a criminal record for serious offences increased by 14 percentage points, suggesting the impact of a father's criminal past is approximately double that of a mother's criminal record on a son's subsequent offending.

There is evidence that a gene-environment interaction is at play in the intergenerational transmission of offending. There is also evidence that a low-risk environment may moderate a genetic predisposition to crime (Goodwin, 2011, 6). Unfortunately, some environments are so foul as to produce extraordinary tragedy as a recent case illustrates. R, a 16-year old youth, was unfit to stand trial for rapes of two children. He was charged with the offence that at a remote Aboriginal community north-east of Kalgoorlie he sexually penetrated a child. R was 13 years of age. The alleged victim was a young girl who was four and a half years of age at the time. An attempt was made to interview R but it was not continued because of a decision that he lacked understanding. R was on bail and living at a hostel in Kalgoorlie. A condition of bail was that he was under the constant supervision of an officer of the Department for Child Protection. Allegedly, in 2011 R sexually penetrated J, an eight-year-old Aboriginal boy who resided in a foster family under the direction of the DCP.

R's mother and father lived in a remote Aboriginal community. It is likely that R was exposed to substances during the antenatal period as his mother reportedly drank alcohol heavily during this time. His early environment was complicated by disrupted attachment, inconsistent parenting, poor supervision, as well as alleged sexual and physical abuse. He grew up with his maternal aunt as well as extended family members.

R had a history of developmental delay with cognitive and language difficulties: and possible traumatic brain injury owing to physical assaults by his biological father. He was provided with a teacher's aide for most of his primary school years. His school reports indicate that he had been disruptive, unable to focus and difficult to engage. His access to stimulation or educational resources had been limited. It seemed that R had become socially alienated and rejected within his own community and family (Children's Court of Western Australia, 2012).

Cannabis

A 2010 longitudinal study of 2,000 adolescents in Norway showed that the use of cannabis was associated with increased level of subsequent receipt of social welfare assistance. Regular cannabis users also received social welfare assistance for longer periods than those who were not using cannabis, or had more infrequent patterns of use. It was less likely that cannabis users would leave the welfare assistance system than those who were not using cannabis. There was no support for a reverse causality process, where receipt of social welfare assistance may support a life-style centred on cannabis (Pedersen, 2011, 1641).

The use of cannabis is frequently noted in cases concerning family breakdown as the following case shows. The matter concerned the parenting of one child, with the father seeking to rest child from mother. The mother had four older children from other relationships. The father had for many years relied upon a disability pension for his income but, from time to time, had undertaken some work. The father had two older children from a previous relationship but as a result of court proceedings he did not see those children. The father explained that his father was a violent alcoholic and the father himself spent time in a boys' home. He was also cared for as a teenager by a family friend.

The father commenced smoking cannabis at about age 13 and used solvents as a teenager. From about age 14 to 16 he occasionally used LSD and mushrooms and then progressed to using speed. The father had acknowledged his extensive criminal history including offences for violence. Cumulatively, he had been incarcerated or institutionalised for 17 years. The father was consumed by his addictions when he met and married the mother.

The mother had received a disability pension since 2010. She was diagnosed with depression, attention deficit disorder, post-traumatic stress disorder and a neck injury. The mother had previously had a diagnosis of bipolar disorder. Her diagnosis of attention deficit disorder and post-traumatic stress disorder stemmed in part from childhood trauma issues including sexual abuse. She attempted suicide at age 12 and had suicidal ideation as an adult. The mother first smoked cannabis at age 12 and she has had a history of heavy cannabis use (Family Court of Australia (a), 2015).

Causes of intergenerational welfare – culture, capacity or class?

Causes of intergenerational welfare dependence are hotly contested. Three leading suspects are a culture of poverty (of which more later), the individual's capacity, or their circumstances. To these may be added the strength of the transmission of attitudes from parents to children. How bad habits and traits are passed on is subject to much debate and research. Why do children with a family history of receiving income-support not show up to school on time? Why is income support related to higher rates of asthma or hospitalisation during childhood? These questions are posed by the best researchers who are, nevertheless, somewhat stumped for answers because parents 'pass a lot of things on to their children... such as values, attitudes and work ethic', which are difficult to observe and measure (Cobb-Clark, 2010, 48).

More perplexing still, debate, at times about causation and transmission, does not lend itself to practical solutions. Whether removing, or indeed enhancing, welfare support removes or enhances adverse attitudes and behaviour is very difficult to know. What is known is that researchers recommend policy that may not be closely related to their conclusions and, at times, is downright wishful thinking. And each policy has attendant risks.

Bad attitudes are passed down, but do they count?

The Youth in Focus Project interviewed 2,400 pairs of young Australians (aged 18) and their mothers about their attitudes towards work, welfare, and what it takes to get ahead in life. The data were linked to almost twelve years of administrative welfare data for these families providing a unique opportunity to assess the role of welfare histories in shaping youths' attitudes.

The study concluded that Australian youths' attitudes to welfare benefits for the unemployed and what it takes to get ahead in life were clearly linked to those of their mothers. Moreover, these attitudes appeared to be shaped by the family's history with the welfare system. Specifically, those growing up in a family with a history of welfare receipt were less likely to oppose the public provision of generous unemployment benefits and less likely to believe that social inequality stems from individual effort and family background than those growing up in non-welfare families. Youths were much more likely to oppose the public provision of generous unemployment benefits and more likely to believe that social inequality stems from individuals' characteristics or family background if their mothers share these views and have a history of employment.

The results supported a 'cultural transmission' model of work-welfare attitudes. Work ethic was also shaped by welfare histories, although there was evidence that welfare intensity may be more important than welfare incidence and that the strength of this relationship depended on which dimension of work-welfare attitudes were considered. There appeared to be a potential for welfare receipt to produce a welfare culture by reducing the work ethic of children. At the same time, there was no evidence that youths' work-welfare attitudes were related to the welfare profiles of others in their neighbourhood. Youths' attitudes towards welfare appeared to be unrelated to their neighbours' welfare receipt suggesting that cultural transmission occured primarily within families rather than neighbourhoods.

The researchers concluded that a history of welfare receipt significantly affected the work ethic of 18-year olds, but cautioned that attitudes were not the same as outcomes and which attitudes were 'most relevant for understanding young people's educational, labour market, and health outcomes' was not clear (Barón, 2008, 24). The general policy implication of these researchers is that getting children away from bad influences is best, for example youth allowances may free the child from the family influence. These insights are consistent with a policy that seeks to limit the opportunity for parents to have children while on a benefit.

Intergenerational maltreatment: drugs and mental health

A study in the United States compared 1,196 caregivers, most of whom were single African American females, and 2,143 children from first- and second-generation child families where abuse had been involved. Reunification of children with the parent was a key measure. All families in the study had a history of substance abuse.

Second-generation families experienced more problems at the time of case opening. Second-generation families had higher rates of neglect and mental health diagnoses compared to first-generation families. Additionally, children from second-generation families were less likely to be reunified within three years even after controlling for problem areas, such as mental health diagnoses and service needs related to housing, domestic violence, and education. The researchers concluded that mental health functioning and generational status went hand-in-hand. That is, it was not just being involved in the child welfare system in a subsequent generation that reduced the chance of reunification, but rather second generation caregivers had more mental health problems (Marshall, 2011, 1028).

This research serves as a reminder that the ability to intervene among parents with drug and mental health problems will be sorely tested and that the possibilities for good outcomes are not good among those in second and subsequent generations. Parents with drug and alcohol problems need help, an aspect of which would be to assist them to control one part of their lives, that is, not to have children while they are dependent on others to live.

Take a recent case to revoke custody orders for children seven years, five years and four years. The Department of Human Services in Victoria sought guardianship for the three children. The oldest had been the subject of a protective application since birth. Children had been placed into the care of a paternal aunt. The paternal aunt's two grandchildren had also lived with her.

The mother was the second oldest of six children. From an early age she displayed aggression, immaturity and poor impulse control, which persisted through primary school. The mother had difficulty forming peer relationships and frequently fabricated stories. She was assessed as having borderline IQ. The mother was a client of DOHS between the ages of 12-18 as a result of frequent absconding from home, stealing to pay for drugs and placing herself at risk by going home with unknown older males. Subsequent to being placed on a custody order, the mother had damaged her family home and other property. The mother had a strong family history of psychiatric illness. Her mother had Bipolar Disorder. Four of the mother's younger siblings had learning disabilities and had each been diagnosed with depression.

The mother had a significant history of substance abuse and had admitted to using illicit substances while she was pregnant with two of her children and while the children were in her care. The father was the second youngest of four children. His parents were both alcoholics. The father had a number of risk factors for neuropsychological impairment. He had several motor vehicle accidents, which may have involved loss of consciousness. He had a 30-year history of variable alcohol intake. He had a history of heroin addiction and use of other illicit substances. He made a self-destructive attempt on his life (Children's Court Victoria, 2007).

Poverty not welfare

Far-reaching reforms of the welfare system of the United States occurred in the early 1990s through the federal *Personal Responsibility and Work Opportunity Reconciliation Act* 1996. These were aimed at promoting adult employment and reducing long-term dependence on welfare. While the details varied from state to state, common policy innovations included time limits, job subsidies, work requirements, and increased funding for child support. Most of the research found substantial increases in the labour force participation of single mothers and reductions in public assistance (Miller, 2012, 463). Nevertheless, there was much disquiet about the impact on some families and women.

One study examined differences between young, single mothers who received welfare and young, single mothers who were poor but did not receive welfare. Data from the 1968 to 1997 Panel Study of Income Dynamics involved 5,000 single mother families and 18,000 children. Overall, the long-term economic well-being of young benefit recipients appeared to be no worse (or better) than non-recipients who started out with low income for an extended period. It appeared to be the persistence of poverty early in adulthood rather than welfare receipt itself that best predicted the likelihood of later life poverty. Single mothers who were poor for a substantial period early in adulthood were as likely to find themselves in or near poverty in later life as single mothers who received benefits for a substantial period at the same time of their lives (Vartanian, 2004, 124).

The authors argued for policy that concentrated on lifting young single women with children out of poverty early in adulthood, rather getting women off welfare (and into work). This study is useful for those who want to engage in chicken and egg arguments about poverty and welfare. The authors' concern was to lift young women out of poverty. The authors acknowledged that the women were poorly prepared for work and that their immediate concerns were with their circumstances, not the future. The women were responding to immediate incentives, and well-trodden pathways, to become a mother. But, rather than attempt direct policies of keeping them at school and not pregnant, they instead argued to design a society where plentiful, interesting and well-paid jobs were available to all. Indeed, these jobs would need to be so attractive as to outbid all other incentives to make bad decisions, such as having a child while on a benefit. Simply wishing that someone were not poor is not a solution. Whatever may be ideological predilections towards blaming the system and not the poor, the tools for intervention are not vast and inexhaustible. Helping dependent people to control their fertility may be the most practical way to hand some modicum of power to the poor.

Not culture, but family planning would help

A further study, based on the United States National Survey of Families and Households (1987 and 1993, sample 13,017 18 years and older), suggested that the vast majority of those previously dependent on welfare were now working, and those who were not working or returned to welfare after working have done so not because of 'cultural effects' but largely as a result of poor schooling, limited work history, substance abuse, depression, disability, or other barriers to employment. So what to do for those who fail to return to work? The authors were satisfied that no culture of poverty existed and that class was the problem. They were nevertheless sufficiently realistic to acknowledge that 'such people would benefit from family planning and programs that enhance the marital and parenting skills of high-risk families' (Bartholomae, 2004, 808).

Others have found that policies that increased the employment of welfare mothers in the United States had positive consequences for younger children, but adversely affected adolescents possibly to be attributed to the reduction in time that parents had to monitor and supervise their adolescent children. The preferred intervention was 'effective parenting', in particular involvement of fathers (Cobb-Clark, 2009, 22). These suggestions around family planning and enhancing parental skills are at least more immediate than tackling the myriad issues that appear to be associated with intergenerational poverty. Tackling intergenerational poverty by tackling poverty may seem sensible, but is a blind alley.

And, indeed, there are risks in tackling any parts of the intergenerational poverty problem. For example, the number of children living with neither biological parent is growing in the United States with foster care caseload rising from 269,000 in 1983 to 429,000 in 1991. The question was whether welfare to work reform would help. The study was based on a 1992 sample (2,808 single parents with 5,666 children) from the Survey of Income and Program Participation. The reform was designed to move single parents into work. The survey found that when state governments reduced the availability of cash benefits, single parents were more likely to organise alternative living arrangements for children.

In other words, there are risks in 'forcing' people off welfare, especially if the recipient fails to gain work and is worse off. The knock-on effect may be that a single parent family has to adapt by shared housing or cutting expenditures to lower the costs of raising children, or, alternatively, to increase the amount of income per remaining child. The researchers concluded that 'reducing the number of children who place demands on household resources is an adaptation used by single families to cope with extreme economic deprivation' (Brandon, 2001, 16). Programs in Australia designed to move parents into work – parenting payment recipients who have a youngest child aged 6 or over must seek work – have been successful in raising the level of workforce participation among single parents. The risks associated with moving people off welfare can and should be managed. The poor and/or welfare recipients having fewer children could as readily achieve relief from the pressure of poverty as an increase in benefits.

Conclusion

For those keen never to blame poverty on the poor, but on 'structures' in society, there is a real lack of policy responses available. Welfare may not be the problem at the heart of intergenerational welfare dependence, and 'the poor' and their behaviour may not be at the heart of intergenerational poverty, but research that promotes widespread 'solutions' to intergenenrational poverty, or ignores the poor's role in their saviour, has nothing much to offer, at least no more than has already been tried in Australia for many years.

The sad truth, 'that there may be little long-term mobility out of the income support system', is countered by some good news, that 'a large proportion of total income support receipt is concentrated among relatively few families' (Pech, 2000, 50). As much as policy-makers can attempt to remake society, by transferring money and opportunity to those on welfare, only if those on welfare can take advantage of the programs can they hope to succeed. Families mediate the experience of welfare – perhaps some better clues lie in those families.

4

What happened to families

Second demographic transition

A very large clue to the causes of intergenerational welfare can be found outside the welfare system. It can be found in family formation. My parents' generation, born early in the 20th century, would be shocked to observe changes to family life now common in the West. While they lived through the tail end of what is known as the 'first demographic transition', which began early in the 19th century and continued into the early 20th century in the West and was defined by declines in mortality and fertility, the 'second demographic transition' was a leap into the dark. It began around 1960 and included postponement of parenthood and marriage, low marriage rates, high divorce rates, high cohabitation, rise of non-marital childbearing, parents having children to different partners, and the extraordinary growth of one-parent families.

There are also new trends emerging along class lines within these broader changes. Educated couples may cohabit, but in time marry and have children in the marriage and maintain stable relationships. Those with less education, lower incomes and perhaps on welfare are more likely to drift into parenthood, may not marry, or, if so, more likely divorce, and marry or cohabit again to have another family. These are not hard and fast rules; they are simply tendencies, but their consequences for family life are great. Public policy responses need to understand them.

Figure 4.1. Total fertility rate, Australia, 1933-2013

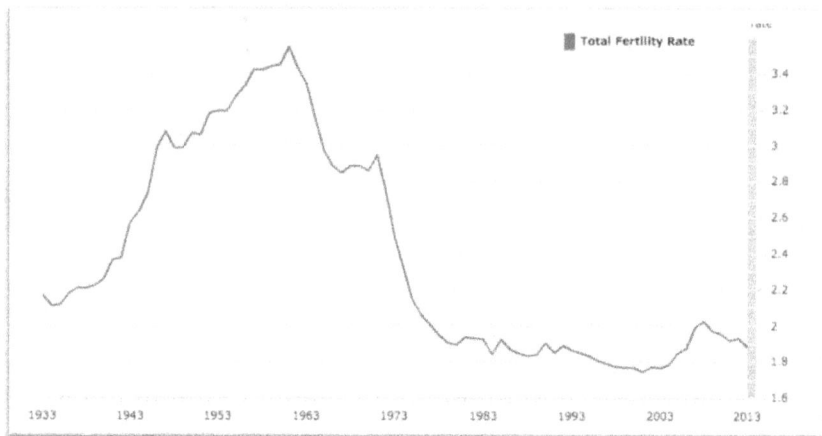

Source: (ABS (b), 2014)

These dramatic changes to family life occurred in the general context of a strong decline in fertility, as shown in figure 4.1. In 2013, Australia's total fertility rate was 1.9 babies per woman. In 1934, it was 2.1, rising to 3.5 in 1961 before falling to 2.9 in 1971 and 1.9 in 1980, remaining reasonably stable since. Within the overall downward fertility rate, the fertility rate changed dramatically for different age groups reflecting three different themes. Teenage pregnancy, for example, rose from a rate (expressed as births per 1,000 women) of 26 in 1933, peaked at 56 in 1971 and fell to 15 in 2013. The peaks for 20-24 year olds and 25-29 year olds were reached in 1961 (226 and 221) and fell to 52 and 100 respectively in 2013, the latter reflecting the fact that women are delaying childbearing. In addition, and reflecting delayed childbearing in an overall decline in fertility, the peaks for 30-34 year olds were 132 in 1946 and 131 in 2008. The peaks for 35-39 year olds were 78 in 1946 and 72 in 2008 (ABS (b), 2014).

The factors at play in the second transition were both cause and consequence of the decline in fertility. New attitudes, new economies, new medicine, new families combined to create fertility rates lower than those witnessed in the midst of the Great Depression, delayed fertility rates not witnessed for half a century and, in the case of teenage pregnancy, low levels never before achieved. Nevertheless, there were 10,407 teenage births in Australia in 2013, mostly ex-nuptial.[21] Raising fertility rates to post-Depression and post-Second World War levels is not a widely shared policy goal, nor is it the purpose here. Rather, the purpose is to provide the context within which dramatic changes in family formation have been expressed and raise some of the associated issues relevant to intergenerational welfare that have emerged as a consequence.

Marriage down and delayed, divorce rates steadying

Australia's marriage rate decreased from 7.2 marriages per 1,000 estimated resident population in 1986, to 5.1 in 2013.[22] In addition, people are delaying marrying. The median age at marriage in 2013 was 32 years for males and 30 years for females, up from 29 and 26 in 1993. Since 1993, the age-specific marriage rate for males between 20-29 years of age has decreased, and has increased for males between 30-39 years of age. Since 1993, the age-specific marriage rate for females between 20-24 years of age has decreased, and has increased for females between 25-34 years of age.

Australia's divorce rate was 2.1 divorces per 1,000-estimated resident population in 2013. In 1971, prior to the *Family Law Act* 1976 (Cth), which made applications for divorce a non-contestable matter, the rate was one. The rate jumped to 4.5 in 1976 and slowly decreased thereafter. In 2013, the median age of males and females at divorce was 45 and 42 years respectively (ABS (a), 2014, 1).

Between 2012 and 2013, the number of children affected by

---

21 Australian Bureau of Statistics, *Births, Australia, 2013*, Table 8.1 'Births, nuptiality and age of mother.'

22 Marriage and divorce rates, known as crude rates, are calculated as the number of marriages or divorces granted during a calendar year per 1,000 estimated resident population at 30 June of the same year.

divorce has decreased from 45,000 to 42,000. The average number of children for divorces involving children decreased to 1.8 children per divorce (ABS(a), 2014, 3). Between 2006-07 and 2012-13, the proportion of adults whose parents had divorced or separated during their childhood (before they turned 18) increased from 15 per cent to 18 per cent (ABS (a), 2015, 7).

Rise of cohabitation

The change in family formation in Australia, the United States and nearly every country in Europe during the past few decades has been astounding. All have experienced declines in marriage and increases in cohabitation and child-bearing outside of marriage (Perelli-Harris, 2014, 1044). In 2012-13 in Australia, 46 per cent of all those currently in a registered marriage cohabited with their partner prior to marriage. The comparable figure in 2006-07 was 39 per cent; in 1975 it was 16 per cent. Of the 2.1 million people over the age of 18 years who were in a de facto marriage in 2012-13, 45 per cent expected to enter into a registered marriage with their current partner. Almost 27 per cent of people over the age of 18 currently in a de facto marriage did not expect to enter into a registered marriage with their current de facto partner. Around 22 per cent of people in a de facto marriage did not know whether they would enter into a registered marriage with their partner (ABS, 2015, 7).

Of those registering a marriage in 2013, 77 per cent cohabited.[23] In table 4.1, comparable figures are shown for Australia, some European countries and the United States, which places Australia at about the rate experienced in West Germany.

---

23 This figure is significantly higher than 'all those currently in a registered marriage', which includes earlier cohorts where the incidence of cohabitation was less.

Table 4.1. Cohabitation in Australia, Europe and United States

Country	Percentage to have ever cohabited
Italy	14 per cent
Poland	17 per cent
United States	50 per cent
Russia	52 per cent
Netherlands	64 per cent
United Kingdom	67 per cent
West Germany	73 per cent
Australia	*77 per cent*
Norway	80 per cent
East Germany	82 per cent

Sources.(ABS (a), 2014; Perelli-Harris, 2014; Sawhill, 2014)

The European figures were based on a cohort of women born in 1970-79 and interviewed between 2003-09. The United States figure was based on surveys of men and women reported in 2006-10.

The reasons why people cohabit are of interest. A unique study, based on focus group discussion with men and women aged 25-40 across 10 countries, including Australia, suggests that the levels of cohabitation were related to culture. Poland has very Catholic traditions and Italy, in addition, has strong traditions of family. The Australian informants were similar to the English in that while living together with someone was not taboo, marriage was still considered an ideal, with the expectation that marriage would be for life (Perelli-Harris, 2014, 1058). Three main concepts to emerge from the study were commitment, testing, and freedom. The Australian attitudes are, in the main, here reported.

Commitment

In Australia, informants used terms such as 'one hundred per cent commitment' or 'life-long union' to indicate that the commitment level in marriage went beyond that of cohabitation. One Australian informant admitted:

My superficial instinct, and it is a horrible judgment and even to
say it out loud it just sounds, like it's against everything I actually
believe, but if somebody said this is my wife or this is my girlfriend,
if you're asking me specifically how do I judge their commitment I'm
always going to assume that wife is more committed than girlfriend.

In several countries, the fear of commitment associated with marriage was one reason given that cohabitation had become more prevalent during the past few decades. Men, in particular, were mentioned as having a fear of commitment in Australia, eastern and western Germany, the Netherlands, the United Kingdom, and Norway. In most of these countries, informants recounted scenarios of friends (or even themselves) not wanting to commit to marriage, even though their girlfriends did.

Some participants disagreed that cohabitation meant a lack of commitment. Long-term cohabitors, sometimes called 'ideological cohabitors', were present in Australia. These informants often asserted that 'marriage was just a piece of paper' or objected to the idea that their commitment within a cohabiting union was less than those who were married.

Testing

Terms such as 'trial marriage', 'test' or 'test period' arose frequently. Regardless of how widespread cohabitation has become, this period of living together unmarried has emerged as a way to try out the relationship. In general, testing was seen as a benefit, allowing the partners to get to know each other and learn each other's habits. From this viewpoint, testing is oriented towards relationship building and alleviates the risk of divorce. In Australia informants advised that people 'try before you buy':

I think that's important, because when you live together a lot of
things you won't see when you were dating because you live apart ...
his habits, what he likes to eat, what he doesn't like to eat, what he
likes to do in the bathroom... you can't imagine it until you really

live together, and then you have to start thinking of how you're going to cope with it.

Freedom

In many ways freedom is the opposite side of the coin from commitment and simply implies that cohabitation is what marriage is not. In Australia, some women felt that finances were less likely to 'get so intertwined' in cohabiting relationships, making it easier for women to maintain a higher level of independence both within relationships and after they broke down.

In the Netherlands, Australia, Western Germany, and the United Kingdom, the discussion of freedom implies more of an emphasis on individualisation, personal freedom, freedom to travel, and women's independence. European and Australian focus group participants rarely mentioned the need for economic stability before marriage. This brings into question whether increasing uncertainty associated with temporary employment and job instability explains the increase in cohabitation outside of the United States.

Non-marital childbearing and one-parent families

Allied with the rise of cohabitation, whether as trial marriage or as the new norm in relationships for having a family, post-Second World War saw a 'weakening of parental oversight of courtship', a 'fundamental trigger to the broader rejection of normative and institutional values that underpinned the second demographic transition.' Changes in values were also reflected in denying the unmarried access to oral contraception and then relenting in the face of demands from a younger generation, and in abortion law reform (Carmichael, 2014, 609).

In time, families began to form around a mixture of non-marital births and premarital and/or maritally conceived births. The 'shotgun' wedding became a relic. In Australia, less than 10 per cent are likely to marry as a result of conception. 'Marriage due to pregnancy had been emphatically rejected at all reproductive ages' (Carmichael, 2014, 624), as a consequence, ex-nuptial births continue to climb.

Table 4.2. Births registered, Australia, 2003-13

Births	2003	2013
Nuptial births	171,853	202,046
Ex-nuptial births	79,308	106,019
Ex-nuptial as per cent of all births	32 per cent	34 per cent

Source: (ABS (b), 2014)

As shown in table 4.2, in 2013, ex-nuptiality in total births in Australia was 34 per cent. Paternity was not acknowledged in three per cent of ex-nuptial total births. By contrast, ex-nuptiality in births to Aboriginal mothers was 87 per cent.[24] Paternity was not acknowledged in 18 per cent of ex-nuptial births to Aboriginal mothers (ABS (b), 2014, table 11.8).

As a separate but related phenomenon, and whether because couples failed to endorse their relationship through marriage, or because relationships have become less enduring and separation and divorce ensues, the proportion of one parent families with children of any age has climbed, and levelled to, in 2009-10, 14 per cent (ABS (a), 2011, 2).

One-parent families were predominately lone mother families (16 per cent of all families with children aged zero to 17 years) rather than lone father families (3 per cent of all families with children aged zero to 17 years). This proportion of lone mother and lone father families has stayed relatively stable since 2006-07. There is an historical aspect to the one-family tale. Not all are young parents. The highest proportion of one-parent families comprised those where the youngest resident child was aged 25 years and over (23 per cent), compared with nine per

24 Nuptial includes traditional Aboriginal and Torres Strait Islander marriages.

cent of couple families for the same age group (ABS (a), 2015, 4).

Nevertheless, of the five million children aged zero to 17 years in 2012-13, one million (21 per cent) had a natural parent living elsewhere. Of these children, 75 per cent lived in one-parent families, 10 per cent in step-families and 12 per cent in blended families. Children were more likely to live with their mother than their father after parents separated.

Figure 4.2. Projected growth in one-parent families, Australia, 2011-36

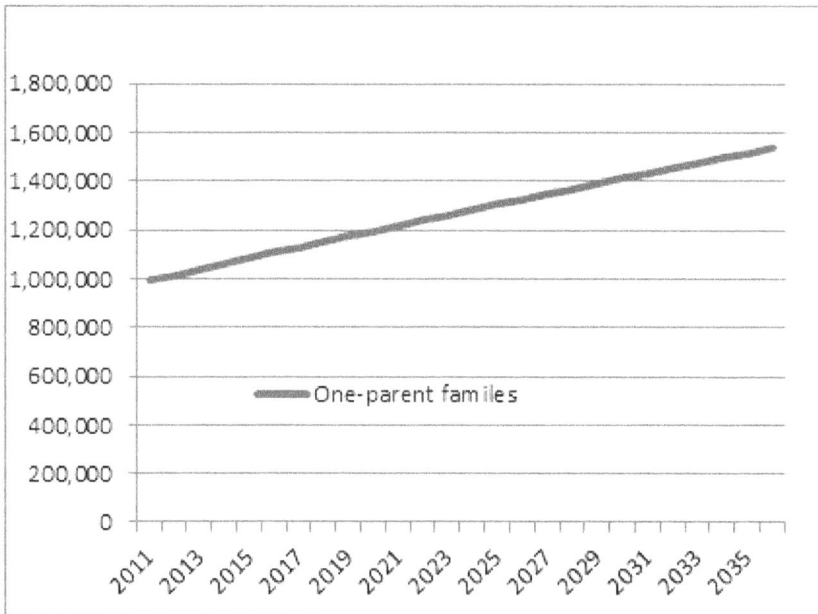

Source: ABS (2015, (b)), *Household and Family Projections Australia, 2011-2036*, Canberra

In 2012-13, 45 cent of children aged zero to 17 years with a natural parent living elsewhere (501,000) saw this parent at least once per fortnight, while 26 per cent rarely saw them (less than once per year or never). As children aged, the likelihood of having at least fortnightly contact with their natural parent living elsewhere decreased. In 2012-13, 54 per cent of children aged zero to 9 years, 43 per cent of children aged 10 to 14 years and 35 per cent of children aged 15 to 17 years saw their natural parent living elsewhere at least once a fortnight (ABS (a), 2015, 6).

The result of these various trends in family formation is the growth of one-parent families. The number of one-parent families in figure 4.2 is projected to increase by 47 per cent over the period 2011-36, from one million to between 1.5 and 1.7 million. In 2011, a female headed 83 per cent of one-parent families. This ratio is projected to remain at a similar level between 2011 and 2036. The number of families in Australia is projected to increase from 6.1 million in 2011 to nine million in 2036, representing a growth of 46 percent.

At the extreme, broken families may have tragic consequences as the inquest into the deaths of two 16 year-olds in Mackay shows. JE was one of seven children. His father left the family home and moved to Sydney when JE was aged seven. JE's mother struggled to cope with the care of the children. JE spent periods of time in the care of other family members, including his maternal grandmother and various aunts and uncles. The relevant Queensland department was involved with JE and his family. Its review identified numerous risk factors, which included an extensive history of drug and solvent use from an early age, poor school attendance, a significant history of offending and criminal behaviour and involvement with the youth justice system. JE was in the youth detention centre in Townsville. JE and his siblings were placed in voluntary care after his mother indicated she was unable to stop them from sniffing paint.

JJ was the youngest of five children. He lived with his mother and brother, who was one year older than he. Prior to his death, JJ's mother was employed [elsewhere] and, as a consequence, JJ and his brother would spend most of their time alone. Like JE, JJ had extensive involvement with the youth justice system. He was first placed on probation at the age of 10. His offending behaviour continued and he received a total of 17 supervised orders and detention orders. He had been remanded in custody at the Townsville Youth Detention Centre. He had been in youth detention on remand for a period of four months. He was sentenced in relation to the violent assault of a 16 year-old male in Mackay. Youth Justice noted that many young men involved in the youth justice system lacked suitable male role models (State Coroner Queensland (b), 2015).

Parents having children to different partners

Australian data suggests an estimated 12 per cent of men, and 16 per cent of women, who were born between 1960 and 1968 and who have two or more children, have had children in more than one marriage. Further, for the most recent generation, around eight per cent of people who have had two or more births have had them outside of marriage. It is not known whether these births occurred in a cohabiting relationship, although given that cohabitation is fairly well accepted in Australia this is likely. Nevertheless, a substantial percentage of people in the youngest generation are having children in more than one relationship (Gray, 2008, 7).

A fascinating and recent study compared mothers' experience of having children with more than one partner in two 'liberal welfare regimes' (Australia and the United States) and two 'social democratic regimes' (Sweden and Norway). Despite quite different arrangements for social welfare, the determinants of childbearing across partnerships were very similar. Women who had their first birth at a very young age or who were less well educated were most likely to have children with different partners. The risk of childbearing across partnerships increased dramatically in all countries from the 1980s to the 2000s, and educational differences also increased, again, in both liberal and social democratic welfare regimes (Thomson, 2014, 485). There are a number of reasons why women have children with more than one partner. High cohabitation and divorce rates are clear signs of instability in adult relationships, often made more difficult during childbearing and rearing years. In addition, single parents are likely to seek new partners, and new couples are likely to want children together. With an increasing pool of single parents and their desire to form new partnerships, it is not surprising that more women are having children in different partnerships.

The Thomson study readily acknowledges that families continue to be a foundational unit in the social order of most societies, and the parent-child bond remains fundamental among kin relationships. In the recent past, children were likely to be reared in the family unit in which married mothers and fathers shared a residence with their biological offspring, generally living apart from extended kin. The rise in divorce in the late twentieth century called into question the viability of the nuclear family model for organising the care and well-being of family members.

When parents did not live together, and when they formed step-families with a new partner, norms, authority, legal relationships, and habits changed. Changing partners when children are involved has profound implications for the character of intra-familial relationships and broader kinship networks. The birth of children in the new partnership adds considerably to that complexity, with possible adverse effects on parents' ability to provide effective parenting and sufficient economic resources for their children. For example, the amount of time it takes for separation, re-partnering, and childbearing with a new partner means that half-siblings are, on average, further apart in age than full siblings. Half-siblings on the mother's side are likely to live together, while those produced by fathers will usually meet less frequently, if at all (Thomson, 2014, 487).

Multi-partner families make life very complicated and sometimes tragic. The multi-partnering is most probably not so much a cause of strife, as a consequence. This is demonstrated by a case involving a mother of nine children. The mother had these nine children from three fathers. Seven of the children were the subjects of protection applications. Mr R had sexually assaulted the eldest daughter. Mr P was the father of the five eldest children. Next was a daughter who had a different father whose identity was unknown to the court. The three youngest were all the children of Mr R. Protection applications were not taken out in relation to two children as they lived with their father at the time the Department of Human Services in Victoria became involved.

There was no criticism of the mother's day to day care of the children. The Department submitted that the children were in need of protection because her de facto, Mr R, had sexually assaulted her eldest daughter, H, and that the mother had failed to support and protect H, which created a risk of future harm to her other children. Mr R was sentenced to seven years imprisonment with a five year minimum for charges of aggravated rape, rape, abduction, indecent assault and intentionally/recklessly cause injury (Children's Court Victoria (b), 2009).

Another case illustrates the extraordinary propensity of couples to change partners and continue to have children, when the original children were not cared for. The case concerns three children five years, two years, and one year and their mother and father, and a protection application for the children.

Mother of the three had three older children, 13 years, 12 years, nine years from a previous relationship for which she was the custodial parent. The father of those children threatened to have them removed from her care and they lived with that father. These three children were the subjects of a report to Department of Human Services Child Protection. The father had five other children, 23 years, 21 years, 20 years, 18 years, and seven years. The mother had seven siblings and half-siblings. The father had five siblings. The mother and father were ordered to submit to random supervised alcohol and drug testing once per week and provide the results to DOHS.

The mother had done some paid work, mainly fruit and vegetable picking, but she had not been in paid employment for many years and had struggled to support her family on her Supporting Parents' Benefit. The mother had a long history of significant mental health problems. The mother had been a very long-standing user of marijuana. The father reported a long history of substance abuse, mainly involving cannabis and alcohol. The condition of the house prior to their placement in care was described thus: 'In my opinion

the house wasn't liveable. There were clothes, scraps, and dog
faeces in the bedroom. The children didn't have a floor to play on'
(Children's Court Victoria (a), 2009).

Men and women at work

Families may be changing because the dominant economic role of
men as breadwinners has changed. That some men are finding regular
and sufficient employment difficult, and many women are taking to
the workforce in greater numbers, may be sources of tension in a
relationship.

There may be segments of the labour force to which these
generalisations apply, but the picture has not changed for some
time for the labour market in Australia as a whole. The labour force
participation rate for women increased from 62 per cent to 65 per
cent between 2004 and 2014. In the same period, the rate for men
remained steady at 78 per cent. The proportion of men who were
employed part-time increased from 12 per cent to 14 per cent, and for
women remained steady at 43 per cent. The hours worked per week
remained steady throughout for men and women and for full and
part-time workers. The unemployment and underemployment rates
in the period were steady for both men and women and full and part-
time.

It is probable that labour force participation and, as important,
women's participation in education, especially post secondary, is a
more accurate indicator of the changing relativities between men and
women. In 2001, 78 per cent of men (20-24 years) attained year 12
or certificate II or above; and in 2014, it was 83 per cent. In the same
period women attained 81 per cent and 90 per cent respectively. Major
changes have occurred at the Bachelor or above levels (18-24 years).
In 2001, enrolments for men were 21 per cent and in 2014 were 25
per cent. In the same period, enrolments of women were 26 per cent
and 34 per cent respectively.[25] Women are beginning to outperform

---

25 Australian Bureau of Statistics, *Gender Indicators, Australia*, Feb 2015. http://

men in the education arena and presumably these qualifications will, in time, be reflected in employment outcomes. The likelihood is that the conversation between men and women will continue to change around earning and caring roles.

Marriage markets

A study of families across hundreds of years and in many countries concluded that 'social mobility is slow, is strongly inherited within families, and that there is little evidence of our ability, using feasible social programs, to increase it' (Clark, 2014, 274). That rather sombre conclusion should not come as a great surprise. Despite the second demographic transition, families are still the crucible of child rearing. The trouble is, so many children are no longer raised within the most propitious of family circumstances.

Some of this is not new. It has been the case for some time, and remains so, for example, that more highly educated women have fewer children (ABS, 2008, 5). The consequences are significant. Children from small families generally fare better than children from large families, at least in educational attainment, income earned, and accumulation of wealth (Parr, 2006, 19). It is not, however, small families alone that counts, but the ability to remain in a relationship for raising children that is vital. That ability has a strong class bias that plays out in the marriage stakes.

In *Marriage Markets: how inequality is remaking the American family*, June Carbone and Naomi Cahn recount numerous changes to family life in America, almost all of which are common to Australia, except for two matters. 'The percentage of children growing up in single parent households is the highest in the developed world'; and 'economic inequality is remaking the American family along class lines, [so that] families are not going through the same changes together' (Carbone, 2014, 1). Their thesis is that rising inequality in the United States has affected men more than women, and that a greater number of

www.abs.gov.au/AUSSTATS/abs@.nsf/Lookup/4125.0Main+Features1Feb%20 2015?OpenDocument accessed 3 October 2015.

educated men are eager to pair with 'high status women' but that a number of poorly educated men no longer play productive roles in an economy that has few jobs for their skills.

In *Generation Unbound: drifting into sex and parenthood without marriage*, Isabel Sawhill recounts very similar facts to those of Carbone and Cahn. Sawhill, while agreeing that there is a growing class divide in family characteristics, notes that more than half of all births to young adults in the United States occur outside of marriage, and are mostly unplanned. Rather than blame economic inequality, Sawhill emphasises the difference between 'planners', who are marrying and having children after establishing careers, and 'drifters', who are having unplanned children early, outside of marriage, and without the stable support of a second parent. This divide, she argues, contributes to rising inequality and decreased social mobility for both young parents and their children (Sawhill, 2014, 2).

An insight of the position of men is gleaned by a recent United States study of 171 low-income non-custodial fathers. Typically, the men had 'at least an ambivalent desire to father and perceive considerable benefits to doing so.' However, they face serious obstacles in meeting societal norms they espouse about the circumstances under which it is appropriate to have a child. Nor do they have much confidence that these obstacles are likely to dissipate, at least during the prime family-building years. It appears that the majority of fertility among low-income men, especially those who are unmarried, is unintended. Fatherhood nevertheless appears to be a powerful and deeply desired source of meaning and identity.

Disadvantaged fathers are aware of the social unacceptability of bearing children in their constrained circumstances, but are also aware that they might never be able to have a child under conditions that are in conformity with society's standards, which is why so many seem to leave pregnancy to chance. The appeal to 'accidental' pregnancy might actually be a way for these men to claim 'a modicum of respectability', by embracing the unintended pregnancy and striving to be involved with their child (Augustine, 2009, 113).

The number of children born outside marriage in Australia, 34 per cent, is of similar concern, if not proportions, to the United States (50 per cent). The other figure quoted in the Sawhill study, that most births are unplanned, may be comparable to the Australian figure. It is that half of those nearly 70 per cent of Australian women of reproductive age using a contraceptive have 'an unplanned pregnancy' (Stopes, 2006, 4).

As for Australian marriage markets, these are not so easily understood or measured. It is not new that the top end marries each other, and the bottom end marries each other with some assortive mating in the middle. It is not clear that the case has ever been different, except that the very large middle section of citizens is not overly distinguished by class attributes. Moreover, there is in Australia and the United States a great deal of upward mobility. What the term, 'marriage market' may portray more accurately is the fact that with new family norms only those at the top can approach the old ideal: a planned, two-parent, stable family.

The class or, more accurately, class and race differences fit the United States mould. The Thomson study found that a mother's education was inversely associated with the risk of a birth with a different father than that of prior children. In Australia, the only educational difference found was a lower risk of childbearing with a different father among women with tertiary education. There was a clear increase from the 1970s onward for childbearing with different fathers. The least well-off were the most likely to have children with more than one partner in all four countries – Australia, United States, Sweden, Norway – examined in the study; these differences have increased over time. The study concluded, that 'childbearing across partnerships may be an important aspect of growing inequality and may suggest the need for new policy supports and interventions' (Thomson, 2014, 504).

Class differentials in marriage, divorce and childbearing behaviour compound the potential transmission of advantage and disadvantage from one generation to the next (Heard, 2011, 125). Separate marriage markets operate because men and women tend to seek partners within their own social circles. Educational attainment exerts a particularly powerful and increasing influence over mate selection, and educational homogamy compounds the potential for advantage and disadvantage to be transmitted from one generation to the next. In addition to the socioeconomic advantages enjoyed by the children of married and well-educated parents, these children are themselves more likely to marry. Conversely, in addition to the privation experienced by children from low socioeconomic backgrounds, these children are more likely to live in one-parent families, with all the attendant disadvantages already described. In turn, they are less likely to form stable partnerships themselves, and more likely to become lone parents.

Multi-generational disadvantage is inextricably intertwined with patterns of family formation. Carbone and Cahn, and Sawhill, observe the polarisation of family formation in the United States. Social and economic inequalities in Australia, although arguably less stark, may yet be sufficient to produce divergent family outcomes such that 'the life chances of children vary according to the socioeconomic resources available to their parents' (Heard, 2011, 139).

Conclusion

Family formation in Australia has changed and it may not be possible to put Humpty Dumpty together again. And why would Australian society want to return to unhappy marriages and women bearing large numbers of children when they did not necessarily wish it. Women are choosing to lead much broader lives beyond childbirth; indeed, the time now spent caring for a family is a diminishing part of a long life. Some parts of society can cope with the changes – feminism, female careers, sex outside marriage, equal partnerships and so on – other parts cannot. A mountain of re-education appears not to have done the job, and cutting benefits to somehow discourage multi-partner childbearing would cause too much pain and, by all accounts, be ineffective.

The earliest intervention, compulsory LARCs, which is relatively benign, and can be administered at no cost to beneficiaries and little cost to the taxpayer, may help. It is likely to place the most vulnerable parents, but especially women, in a position where they can plan a family. Business-as-usual has very unhappy results as court case after court case attests.

5
Many remedies …
little progress

Plenty of policies, no prevention

There is plenty of evidence that many people in poor circumstances make poor decisions, decisions that may harm the prospects for improving their circumstances. Having a child while on a benefit is a poor decision. All of the programs designed to patch matters after the birth of a child are proof that, without good parenting, children will struggle to survive in a sophisticated and demanding society. Until proven otherwise, parents are the best people to raise a child, and the best prospects for parents to raise their children are to improve their life chances before they embark on having children. Governments should not interfere with such decisions, except when they are paying a benefit. Here lies the opportunity to give pause, and space to plan, before embarking on parenthood.

Programs designed to solve problems of disadvantage have been in place for a very long time. Nevertheless, intergenerational welfare dependence persists. A very large sum of money has been applied to these issues, and there is little left in the kitty to try any new expensive programs. Australian taxpayers have been generous to those on welfare but Australian government budgets are in deficit. Those who think, or wish, that all would be well if only Australia were a more egalitarian society, should think again. Not only would a more equal society damage the rights of the vast majority to keep what is theirs, there is little evidence that giving more, relative to others, to the welfare dependent solves anything. If it did, the problem would have been solved long ago.

Attitude stands in the way of solving intergenerational welfare: attitude on the part of those on welfare and attitude on the part of those trying to get them off. Sometimes the people you want to help do not want it, or they can be hard to reach, or they respond to immediate incentives and pressures that are not conducive to planning a family. Governments know this and have become more focussed on changing attitudes among beneficiaries through more stringent compliance and greater obligations. Attitudes among policy-makers, however, constrain them from considering policies that effectively change behaviour.

Money – as good as it gets

The Australian tax system is fair. It is fair because Australian electors have, in the course of many elections, arrived at the proposition that the tax system should be progressive, that is, those with a greater ability to pay are expected to pay more than the rest. The progressive taxation system, working in conjunction with a transfer system that distributes taxation to those most in need, is fair indeed.

The net result on Australian incomes after the imposition of taxation and transfer benefits is set out in figure 5.1. The electorate has been divided into ten income groups, from lowest to highest. The higher groups pay a higher percentage of their gross income, which is a much higher absolute amount than those on lower incomes. The higher groups receive no or few cash transfer benefits. The lower groups pay a lower percentage of their gross income, which is a much lower absolute amount than those on higher incomes. The lower groups receive almost all of the cash transfer benefits.

Figure 5.1. Taxpayers and transfer recipients by private income, 2014-15

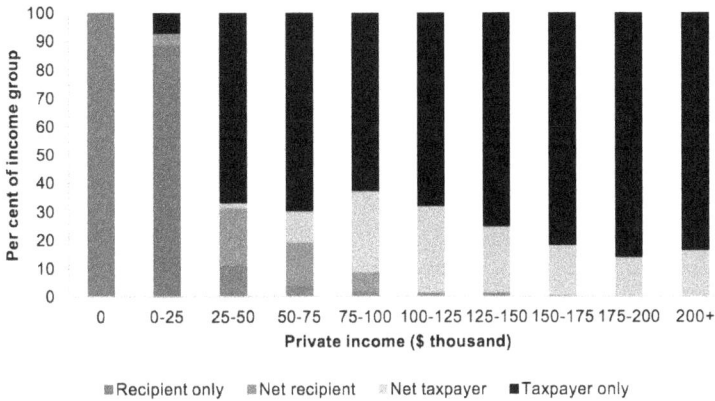

Source: (Productivity Commission (b), 2015, 79)

Concentrating on income tax alone provides a stark contrast of net givers and receivers. For example, an Australian who earns less than $20,000 per year is likely to receive a number of benefits, but pay no income tax. By contrast, someone who earns $100,00 per year may receive no benefits, but will pay $27,000 in income tax, $10,000 of which goes to the welfare of others.[26]

Among those inclined, there is always hope that still more money can be squeezed, if not from individual taxpayers, at least from companies. If only it were so. The company taxation rate in Australia is 30 per cent. The rate in Singapore is 15 per cent, in the United Kingdom is 20 per cent, in Canada, the OECD and China is 25 per cent (Australian Government, 2015, 27). If Australian corporations want to continue to compete and generate wealth for Australians, egalitarians will find little joy and little money in raising company taxes.

Nor will egalitarians find it by borrowing. Australian governments are spending much more than they tax. The Australian Government's deficit is projected to be $35 billion in 2015-16, gross debt is projected to reach $573 billion by 2025-26 (Australian Treasury, 2015). In 2012-13, the Australian Government provided more than $110 billion

---

26 Australian Government, *Budget 2015*, http://www.budget.gov.au accessed 3 October 2015.

in cash transfer payments and around $2 billion for employment services. The estimated cost of administering payments in 2012-2013 was approximately $3 billion (Reference Group, 2015, 70).

Any new policies to overcome welfare dependence will not have much, if any, new money to support them. And, in any event, how far can governments go to make good a person's life? The Scottish government, for example, has legislated that by August 2016, every child or young person will be entitled to a friend: a Named Person (*Children and Young People (Scotland) Act* 2014). The Named Person will be available 'to listen, advise and help a child or young person and their family, providing direct support or helping them to access other services. They can help families address their concerns early and prevent them becoming more serious.'[27]

Early intervention is the hope of the side

The assumption that underlies most programs is that, if every child were brought up in a happy family, and with skilled parents all would be well – not equal, but well. Some would do better than others, either because they were brighter and worked harder, or were more ambitious, or were lucky. Summarising data from the Longitudinal Study of Australian Children, children in families with two resident parents whose family environment becomes more cohesive show improved social and emotional wellbeing. By contrast, children whose family environments become more 'problematic' show increased social and emotional problems (Mullan, 2014). In the absence of happy families and parents with requisite skills, the hope of the side is early intervention, investing in children and their parents' skills.

There is strong support for the idea that children's early years are a fruitful time for intervention to improve educational and achievement outcomes for low-income and disadvantaged children. Full-day, centre-based, educational programs for children who are at

---

27 The Scottish Government, http://www.gov.scot/Topics/People/Young-People/ gettingitright/named-person accessed 22 October 2015.

high risk for school failure, starting in early infancy and continuing until school entry have been shown to generate 'impressive long-term improvements in subsequent education, crime, and employment' (Duncan, 2012, 91). Less intensive programs, for example, those that aim to improve 'the coordination of services for children 0-5 years of age and their families' show little impact (Edwards, 2014, xv).

Australian governments understand these lessons. This is why childcare-early education spending in Australia is mammoth and growing. In 2013-14, total Australian, state and territory government expenditure on early childhood education and care services was $7.7 billion, compared to $6.8 billion (12.5 per cent in real terms) in 2012-13. Nationally, between 2009-10 and 2013-14, the average annual growth rate of real expenditure was 10.6 per cent. In the March quarter of 2014, more than one million children aged 12 years or younger attended Australian government-approved child care services, an increase of 7.6 per cent from 2013 (Productivity Commission, 2015, 3.12 and 3.18).

There is no doubt that targeting can be improved. In 2013-14, representation of children aged zero to 12 years from 'special needs' groups in childcare was lower than their representation in the community nationally. This applied to non-English speaking, Aborigines, low income families, disabled and those in rural and remote areas, although the representation was not overly unbalanced (Productivity Commission, 2015, 3.24). How many billions of dollars it would take to improve the representation of children from special needs groups in child care is moot, having got them there, just how much good it would do is anyone's guess.

Parenting programs

Some parenting programs such as Good Beginnings[28] are funded by the Australian and state governments, but the vast majority of relationship education services in Australia are locally developed,

28 Good Beginnings, http://www.goodbeginnings.org.au/wp-content/uploads/2015/02/Good-Beginnings-Executive-Summary-2pp-printed1.pdf accessed 20 April 2015.

largely undocumented, and have adopted a limited approach in evaluating their service effectiveness (Halford, 2005, 156). A recent foray into the parenting market by the former Minister for Social Services, Kevin Andrews, the taxpayer-funded $200 million marriage counselling voucher program was abolished in July 2015 due to low uptake. Around 10,000 couples had registered for the scheme but only one third of these had attended a relationship education or counselling service.[29]

More enduring is the Triple P – Positive Parenting Program – developed by Professor Matt Sanders at the University of Queensland.[30] The Triple P parenting system is used in 25 countries and has been translated into 17 languages. More than 55,000 practitioners have been trained in its delivery. Numerous research studies have found reliable positive effects of the program for child behaviour problems, parenting behaviour, and parental well-being and relationship quality (Nowak, 2008, 114). There are hundreds of programs available at little or no charge to parents. These are subsidised by governments in NSW and Western Australia, local government, for example City of Greater Geelong, and many not-for-profit and community groups.

Mutual obligations

Early intervention is provided in the context of a wider range of interventions. Those on the dole are required to participate in activities to improve their chances of work. Parents are encouraged to return to the workforce. Some of those in chronic disadvantage have their income 'managed' so that it is not misspent. In addition, in extreme cases, where children are under threat from their family, or the family is unable to care for them, there are systems of child protection and adoption and fostering.

Those in receipt of newstart allowance have an obligation to

---

29 Department of Social Services, https://www.dss.gov.au/our-responsibilities/families-and-children/programmes-services/stronger-relationships-trial accessed 19 July 2015.
30 Parenting and Family Support Centre, https://www.pfsc.uq.edu.au accessed 20 April 2015.

participate in activities that will improve the chances of finding and keeping a job. It is made absolutely plain that it is 'about the efforts you make, in return for your payments' (Department of Human Services (b), 2015, 2). Mutual obligation requirements are contained in an Employment Pathway Plan-Individual Participation Plan. The Plan is negotiated between the recipient and the government official or, more commonly, an employment services provider. The Plan includes activities such as job search, education and training, and work experience activities or other activities to improve the recipient's chances of obtaining a job.

Looking for work includes actively looking for and being willing to accept suitable paid work including full-time, part-time and casual work. It also encompasses applying for jobs – attending job interviews – up to 10 per fortnight may be required (filling out a Job Seeker Diary when required), being willing to undertake any work, attending all appointments when requested. The Australian Government also insists that job seekers on Job Search Allowance attend appointments with employment services providers. The data for 2011-12 suggests that 22 per cent do not comply with their obligation to attend.[31]

Return-to-work

Parenting payment (PP) is an income support payment for both single and partnered parents. It is only payable to one member of a couple. There are effectively two different categories within PP. These are PPS for single parents, and PPP for partnered parents.[32] The objective of the PP is to provide assistance to principal carers with parenting responsibilities, and provide incentives to increase workforce participation for principal carer parents and reduce dependency on income support.

The broad objective of the arrangements, established through an employment pathways plan (EPP), is that people should look for,

---

31 Department of Employment, http://employment.gov.au/job-seeker-compliance-data accessed 24 April 2015.
32 There are 24 types of supplementary assistance available to those on parenting payments.

and undertake, paid work in line with their work capacity. Various considerations are taken into account:

- Education, experience, skills, age, physical condition and health
- State of the labour market
- Availability of places in appropriate courses of education or training
- Transport options available where the person lives
- Family and caring responsibilities
- Financial costs of compliance with the terms of the EPP
- Accommodation situation, and
- Circumstances, for example, a victim of family violence, which may affect the ability to participate.

Mandatory part-time participation requirements apply to PP recipients who:

1. Have a youngest child aged six or older, and
2. Have not been exempted from participation requirements.

If a PP recipient is already subject to part-time participation requirements but has an additional PP child, then the mandatory requirements would not apply until this new youngest child turns six. In the event that an EPP was in operation when the new PP child comes into the person's care (for example, a new child is born), the existing agreement will cease, and a new agreement will not be required until the youngest child turns six.[33]

There have been strides in employment for single mothers. Increasing proportions of women over the last few decades have maintained some attachment to the labour force after having children. In 1983, among couple families, those with a single-income earner clearly predominated, representing almost half the families. By 2012, however, this proportion had fallen to 30 per cent. Single mothers' rates of both full-time and part-time paid work have also increased

---

33 Department of Social Services, http://guides.dss.gov.au/guide-social-security-law/3/5/1/160 accessed 30 April 2015.

during this period. Whereas in 1983, 20 per cent of single mothers had full-time paid work and 12 per cent had part-time paid work, by 2012, the rates were 27 per cent and 29 per cent respectively (Weston, 2014, 80).

The question for Australia in the return to work rules is whether a mother can continue to delay return to work by having subsequent children. In 2011, the New Zealand Government decided to ensure that, where parents have additional children while receiving a benefit, their availability for work expectations would be based on the age of their previous youngest child, once the new-born turned one year of age. In practice this means that if a parent who has a four year-old (or younger) child has another child while on benefit, it will be expected that the mother will be available for part-time work as the four-year-old turns five years of age (provided the newborn is by this time one year old). This group represents more than three-quarters of the subsequent childbirths on benefit. Under previous legislation, parents who had additional children while on benefits were not required to take up employment until the youngest subsequent child was six. The argument was that those rules increased the likelihood that at-risk families were locked into long-term benefit dependence. In some cases, it meant that 'the social and financial advantages of employment [were] denied to families for decades' (NZ MSD (b), 2012, 2).

Evidence from New Zealand was that in 2011, 26,000 women receiving domestic purpose benefits (29 per cent of clients) had included additional new-born children in their benefit at least once since 1993. Parents who have additional children on benefit are a high-risk group. More than 90 per cent, for example, are single. Among beneficiary sole parents, those who have subsequent children on benefits are more likely to have been on benefit from a young age, have started on benefits with a new-born, or have no record of having being employed before, after or during, spells on benefits. Compared to all women receiving the benefit, those who have had a subsequent child in the last year are more likely to be Maori (NZ MSD (b), 2012, 2).

The Australian policy on additional children on benefit needs to follow the New Zealand lead if serial children are to be prevented from being born to parents on benefit.

Income management

The most stringent form of mutual obligation is income management. Income management was initially introduced as part of the Northern Territory Emergency Response in prescribed areas of the Northern Territory. Income management was designed to encourage welfare payments to be used for needs such as housing and food, and to ensure less money is available to spend on alcohol, drugs, cigarettes and pornography. Income management also aimed to protect vulnerable people from financial exploitation, including the practice known as 'humbugging' in some Aboriginal communities. The scheme works by directing a proportion of a welfare recipient's income support and family assistance payments to the purchase of priority items, such as food, clothing and rent.

Legislation for a new model of income management took effect from 2010. Income management initially applied in:
- Northern Territory
- Cape York, Queensland, and
- Designated areas of Western Australia

From 2012, five additional locations were added:
- Playford (South Australia)
- Greater Shepparton (Victoria)
- Bankstown (New South Wales)
- Rockhampton (Queensland), and
- Logan (Queensland).

Income management measures are targeted to specified groups of income support payment recipients, based on their higher risk of social isolation and disengagement, poor financial literacy, and participation in risky behaviour. These groups comprise among others:

- People referred by the Queensland Families Responsibilities Commission
- Disengaged youth who have been receiving benefits for more than 13 weeks out of the last 26 weeks
- Long-term welfare payment recipients who have been receiving benefits for more than 52 weeks out of the last 104 weeks
- People assessed by Centrelink as requiring income management
- Vulnerable youth and those who receive crisis payment due to prison release, and those who reside where income management operates
- People referred for income management by child protection authorities, and
- People referred for income management by other state and territory authorities such as the NT Alcohol Mandatory Treatment Tribunal.[34]

There is some research to suggest that conditional transfers lead to an increase in the welfare of the child (Martinelli, 2003, 540). The question is whether compulsory LARC should be an additional condition applying to this group of recipients, if not others.

Child support scheme

The Child Support Scheme was introduced in 1988 in response to concerns about the adequacy of court-ordered child maintenance and the difficulties that existed in the collection of maintenance in Australia. There were also concerns about the poverty of women

---

34 Australian Government, Guide to Social Security Law, http://guides.dss.gov.au/guide-social-security-law/11/1/1/10 accessed 29 April 2015.

and children following separation and divorce and the increasing government expenditure for maintaining children where their absent parents did not contribute towards their upbringing, so called 'dead beat dads'.

The Scheme is based on the principles of parental responsibility for the financial well-being of children when parents separate or divorce, and limiting government involvement by allocating the costs of raising children in separated families between parents and taxpayers. The parent who does not live with their children because of separation or divorce (the payer) is required to make a financial contribution towards their upbringing. The Government prescribes in great detail who shall receive what in a family that no longer lives together. The contribution is based on the:

- Payer's income and the percentage of that income assessed on the basis of the amount that parent would contribute in an intact family
- Exempt amount of the payer's income for his/her own support when calculating income for child support, and
- Amount of the payee's disregarded income, that is, the amount the payee can earn until it affects the calculation of the child support payment.

The system treats the children of first and second families as equally as possible by using the cost of the children from the second family in determining the child support payable. [35]

Child protection

When early intervention, income support and mutual obligations fail, the state has an obligation and the power to protect children from their parents or carers. Statutory child protection is the responsibility of state and territory governments. Each state and territory department

35 Australian Government, Department of Social Services, https://www.dss.gov.au/our-responsibilities/families-and-children/programs-services/history-of-the-child-support-scheme accessed 29 April 2015.

responsible for child protection provides assistance to vulnerable children who have been, or are at risk of being, abused, neglected, or otherwise harmed, or whose parents are unable to provide adequate care or protection. Children and young people are defined as those aged less than 18. This includes unborn children in jurisdictions where they are covered under the child protection legislation. A number of government and non-government organisations share a common duty of care towards the protection of children and young people.

Departments responsible for child protection investigate, process and oversee the handling of child protection cases. Assistance is provided to children and their families through the provision of, or referral to, a wide range of services. The national recurrent expenditure on child protection and out-of-home care services was about $3 billion in 2012-13, a real increase of $178 million (6 per cent) from 2011-12 (AIHW (b), 2014, 2).

Community members, professionals (for example, police or health practitioners), organisations, children themselves, their parent(s), or another relative may make reports of concern about a child. These reports may relate to abuse and neglect or to broader family concerns, such as economic problems or social isolation. The defined threshold for intervention varies from jurisdiction to jurisdiction, which can lead to differences in the responses taken to initial reports.

Child protection notifications are assessed to determine whether an investigation is required, if referral to support services is more appropriate, or if no further protective action is necessary. The aim of an investigation is to obtain more detailed information about a child who is the subject of a notification and to determine whether the notification is 'substantiated' or 'not substantiated'. Substantiation indicates there is sufficient reason (after an investigation) to believe the child has been, is being, or is likely to be, abused, neglected or otherwise harmed. The relevant department will then attempt to ensure the safety of the child or children through an appropriate level of continued involvement, including the provision of support services to the child and family.

In situations where further intervention is required, the department may apply to the relevant court to place the child on a care and protection order. Court is usually a last resort, for example, where the families are unable to provide safe care, where other avenues for resolution of the situation have been exhausted, or where the extended family is unable to provide safe alternatives for care of children. Some children are placed in out-of-home care because they were the subject of a child protection substantiation and require a more protective environment. Other situations in which a child may be placed in out-of-home care include those where parents are incapable of providing adequate care for the child, or where alternative accommodation is needed during times of family conflict.

At any point in the child protection process, departments may refer children and their families to family support services. Family support services can include programs that seek to prevent the occurrence of family dysfunction and child maltreatment, that provide treatment, support and advice to families, and more intensive programs to assist the most vulnerable families. Family support services may be used instead of, or as a complementary service to, a statutory child protection response. Examples include parenting and household skills development, therapeutic care, and family reunification services (AIHW (b), 2014, 5).

The Queensland Child Protection Commission of Inquiry (2012), led by Tim Carmody QC, found that during the last decade, child protection intakes had tripled, the rate of Aboriginal and Torres Strait Islander children in out-of-home care had tripled, the number of children in out-of-home care had more than doubled, and children in care were staying for longer periods.

In the last decade in Queensland, the budget for child protection services has more than tripled, from $183 million in 2003-04 to $773 million in 2012-13. The reason for the growth is the demand for out-of-home care services. The Commissioner recommended ways in which the department could reduce the costs of out-of-home care. Principal among these was to reduce the extent of over-reporting in order to increase resources on the most likely cases. For example, the Queensland Police Service has a blanket policy of reporting domestic violence incidents where at least one of the parties has a child residing with them. The Commissioner also recommended greater investment in family support and other secondary services, including adoption (Queensland CPCI, 2013, xviii).

Adoption

Adoption is one of several options used to provide permanent care for children unable to live with their families. It is a legal process where rights and responsibilities are transferred from a child's parent(s) to their adoptive parent(s). When an adoption order is granted, the legal relationship between the child and their parent(s) is severed. The legal rights of the adopted child become the same as they would be if the child had been born to the adoptive parent(s). A new birth certificate may be issued for the child bearing the name(s) of the adoptive parent(s) as the legal parent(s), and the new name of the child, if their name is changed.

Adoption was once regarded as a solution for the permanent care of illegitimate babies, the risk of impoverishment for single mothers, and the needs of infertile couples. A high degree of secrecy characterised past practices, based on the notion that, among other things, those involved needed to be protected from the social stigma of illegitimacy. However, during the past few decades, raising children outside registered marriage has become more accepted, and more support has been made available to lone parents. These changes have reduced the pressure on unmarried women to give up their children for adoption.

The secrecy that surrounded past adoptions of Australian children has given way to a system predominantly focused on the needs of the child, characterised by the open exchange of information, with the openness of adoptive parents to discussing adoption-related issues with an adopted child recognised as beneficial for the child's adjustment. Access to the adopted child by parties to an adoption (an 'open' adoption) is facilitated in all states and territories, although the degree to which this occurs varies among jurisdictions (AIHW (a), 2014, 1). The key question is when a child should be adopted. Clearly, some parents are not competent to raise children. Sometimes, a reluctance to intervene, driven by an anti-adoption fashion, has tragic consequences.

Chloe Lee Valentine died on 20 January 2012 in South Australia. She was four years and five months old. Chloe was living in a house with her mother Ashlee Polkinghorne, and Ashlee's partner of the time, Benjamin McPartland. Polkinghorne and McPartland had purchased a 50cc dirt bike for Chloe. McPartland repeatedly put Chloe on the bike despite her being unable to stop the bike without falling off. Chloe was rendered unconscious … Polkinghorne and McPartland waited eight-and-a-half hours before calling an ambulance. McPartland was sentenced to seven years, and Polkinghorne was sentenced to eight years.

There had been many previous warning signs that Polkinghorne was unfit to be Chloe's mother and guardian. The warning signs had been made known to the child protection authority, Families South Australia. It failed in its duty. Ashlee had a boyfriend by the name of Thomas Lagden to whom she became pregnant. She was 'couch surfing' before obtaining a unit provided by the Salvation Army. During Ashlee's pregnancy she was dirty, smelly and unhygienic and known to be taking drugs and drinking. Friends contacted the Child Abuse Report Line (State Coroner South Australia, 2014).

The coroner had been impressed by the work of Jeremy Sammut in relation to the failures in Australian child protection systems and the low reliance in Australia on adoption for children in the child protection system. Sammut has made a case for early statutory intervention and adoption by suitable families. Unfortunately, adoption appears to be a taboo subject in the child protection world (Sammut, 2015).

During 2013-14 only 317 adoptions were finalised. It was the lowest annual number on record. It is a fall of nine per cent from the 348 adoptions in 2012-13, and 76 per cent from the 1,294 adoptions recorded 25 years earlier in 1989-90 (AIHW, 2009, vi). Nevertheless, cases such as Chloe Valentine's death and the remarks by the coroner may suggest a shift in attitudes away from an, at times, blind adherence by department officials to keeping families intact despite the risk to the child. An alternative route to adoption is sole parental responsibility, which can be awarded by the Family Court under certain circumstances, although this generally applies to other family members.

Fostering

Foster care is an alternative to adoption for children and young people who cannot live safely at home with their parents. The foster system, however, is facing severe pressures, with more foster parents leaving than there are new people volunteering. At the same time, demand is increasing, with the number of Australian children in out-of-home care increasing threefold between 1990 and 2010. In 2011, 37,648 children were in out-of-home care throughout Australia. In 2012, there were 6,702 children in care in Victoria, an increase of nine per cent on the previous year. Overall, there was a 40 per cent increase in the number of children placed in out of home care in Victoria from 1997-2012. In 2011, 37 per cent of children were in foster care; 42 per cent were in relative-kin care; 12 per cent were in 'other' home-based care; and nine per cent were in residential care. In 2011, there were an estimated 1,574 Victorian foster parent households who had a placement during the year; 226 foster parents commenced fostering whilst 291 foster parents exited foster care in 2010-11. Over the past two years, the decline in numbers is even more significant, with 806 households exiting foster care compared with 517 commencing (McHugh, 2013, 2).

Fostering can be a blessing when it relieves authorities of the need to open state facilities for childcare. Nevertheless, there are sometimes tragic outcomes in foster care. A recent case involved the Director-General of the NSW Department of Family and Community Services. The consensual parenting orders were not fulfilled – the parties had two young children aged six years and three years respectively. The elder child lived with the father following separation and had been in foster care since late 2011 – the younger child had been in foster care since early 2009.

Neither child had a particularly meaningful relationship with either parent or paternal grandmother. Both children settled well with their foster carers. The mother had a history of forming relationships with violent partners and was inclined to give priority to her need for a relationship above enjoyment of unsupervised time with children.

Both parent's neglected the children's emotional needs – both parents had limited capacity or willingness to facilitate close and continuing relationships between them and the children. Neither parent had capacity to provide for the children's needs on a full-time basis. The father used illicit drugs. There was an unacceptably high risk of harm to children in the care of either parent and sole parental responsibility was allocated to the Minister for Family and Community Services of NSW. Orders were made for the children to spend limited time with the mother, father and paternal grandmother (Family Court of Australia, 2012).

Another case had a tragic outcome. At the time of his death A was six years and five months old and lived with foster carers, Mr and Ms B. A was placed into the custody of the Chief Executive, Department of Communities, Child Safety and Disability Services Queensland. The department noted that at times Mr and Ms B had nine children in their care. On the day of A's death there were eight children in their care (one having left the house that morning). The department considered that the number of children approved to be in the care of Mr and Ms B was excessive and may have affected the level of supervision that Mr and Ms B were able to provide. After the death of A the number of children approved to be in the care of Mr and Ms B was reduced to six (State Coroner Queensland (a), 2015). No system for the out-of-home care of children is completely safe, and fostering has had a history of considerable trauma.

Conclusion

Every dollar in every Australian government budget is spoken for. Indeed, dollars that are not yet in the budget are spoken for. Every dollar has a constituency – pensioners, patients, school children and teachers, the disabled – calling for more. None of these is willing to stand aside for some other need. There is no new money, and a great deal is being devoted to repaying debt from earlier, non-productive borrowing.

And yet professionals are always looking to solve problems with costly interventions. For example, early intervention is the new black. Professionals are prepared to have the taxpayer spend billions of dollars on the employment of professionals to make parents parent. Their hope is that if every child could spend as many hours as possible away from his or her parents, and trained intensively for years and years, all would be well. Many of those same professionals who argue for greater intervention are opponents of the compulsory LARC scheme. Those at the front line – police, lawyers, court officers, and experienced social workers – and a huge section of the public are not. They are fiercely in favour, because they see and understand human frailty as it affects children especially.

6

Blaming the poor and other trash talk

If you want to criticise, read the proposal

The proposition, no contraception, no dole, has attracted a fair amount of criticism, often from those who have never read the original articles. But that rarely stops critics. In all, there are four arguments, critical of the proposal to make LARCs compulsory for some welfare recipients. None of these arguments – inequality, eugenics, breaching human rights, stigmatising and/or blaming the poor – is an accurate or valid criticism of the proposal. A further argument, in favour of the proposal and based on population control, is rejected because it is not an objective of the policy and, in any event, is unlikely to be an outcome of the policy.

Obsessed with inequality

So much of social policy is obsessed with the alleged evils of inequality, as if inequality is a problem in itself and, indeed, is solvable. As Australia has grown wealthier the living standards of the poor have been raised along with all others. Taxi drivers in Brisbane earn a great deal more and live a great deal better than taxi drivers in Bangladesh. In addition, as observed in figure 5.1, Australia transfers very generous amounts of money from rich to poor. It is better to be a pensioner and welfare recipient in Australia than almost anywhere else in the world.

However, the proportions taken from the top and transferred to the bottom are unlikely to change. They are unlikely to change because, if an Australian government did tax the rich to within an inch of their life, rich people would leave or not come to Australia, or lessen their efforts, or avoid taxation, and all would be poorer for it. It is, after all, their money. Moreover, the effectiveness of welfare has limits. While it is expected that persons receiving training assistance expand their capacities, if the value of the extra capacity is less than the cost of the assistance to create it, there is an overall loss of welfare. For example, keeping students at school beyond their ability to learn is a waste of time and money. Getting the best out of every person, which is what equality of opportunity aims to do, depends largely on the person.

A rising standard of living and income mobility are more important than equality. The living standards of all Australians have risen for generations, particularly in the last decade.[36] One reason for progress is that bright or tenacious children from humble, and not so humble, backgrounds can rise to their best abilities. Australia has a good degree of income mobility, not simply because of income transfers from rich to poor, but because broader factors such as well-informed markets, secure property rights, absence of corruption, and rewards for entrepreneurship make the use of talent more likely (Boudreaux, 2014, 237). In Australia, less 'human capital' is wasted than may otherwise occur if Australia were not such an open and liberal society.

All wealthy countries have programs designed to loosen, if not break, the link between parents' background – education and income – and children's opportunities. There is evidence, for example, of a correlation between higher enrolment in childcare and early childhood education with a lower influence of parental socio-economic background on teenager cognitive skills. These policies are likely to be most efficient when targeted at children from low-income families. Universal government loan systems for tertiary education, progressive income taxation and unemployment benefits (the level is subject to

---

36 Australian Bureau of Statistics, http://www.abs.gov.au/ausstats/abs@.nsf/Lookup/1370.0main+features352013 accessed 27 July 2015.

debate) are also associated with higher social mobility (Causa, 2010, 37). Australia has all of these programs.

There is one area, however, in which the welfare state and its many programs appears to fail. Women who had their first birth at a very young age or who are less well-educated are most likely to have children with different partners. The birth of children in the new partnership, potentially, has adverse effects on parents' ability to provide effective parenting and sufficient economic resources for their children. The Thomson study, referred to in chapter four, expected associations between socioeconomic status and childbearing across partnerships to be weaker and possibly absent in countries with more generous welfare provisions, especially those directed toward families with children. The assumption was that social democratic regimes would produce more favourable outcomes to the least well off. However, socioeconomic differences in childbearing across partnerships were not less pronounced or absent in social democratic welfare states. Most important to note in passing is the comment by the authors that, although there had been an increase in economic inequality in Sweden, Norway and the United States, 'in Australia … inequality has been moderate and relatively stable' (Thomson, 2014, 503).

There was no clear evidence from the study that welfare state regime or absolute level of inequality generated the 'diverging destinies' of women from different classes and levels of education in these four countries. In other words, childbearing across partnerships is associated with socioeconomic disadvantage, but more welfare is unlikely to fix the problems associated with childbearing across partnerships. Relationships among the least well educated appear less stable and more likely to produce multiple partnerships and multiple children from them. More money may not help, but better planning may. Inequality is not the enemy. Standing by and watching people make poor choices, indeed, possibly aiding those choices with welfare, serves neither the gods of equality nor the interests of women who make poor choices by using welfare.

Eugenics – not even close

Eugenics is the belief and practice that aims at improving the genetic quality of the human population. It is a social philosophy advocating the improvement of human genetic traits through the promotion of higher reproduction of people with desired traits (positive eugenics), or reduced reproduction and/or sterilisation of people with less-desired or undesired traits (negative eugenics), or both.

A desire to sterilise what were described as the 'unfit' has been a recurring theme in the West since the end of the 19th century. It was part of a popular movement, based on the idea of eugenics, or the use of science to 'improve the race'. A particular criticism of the compulsory LARC proposal is that it presumes that the state is the best judge of who is fit to breed.[37] Precisely, the state is not the best judge of who is fit to breed, but the state is intimately involved already because it, in effect, pays some people to have children. It may be true that 'most developed societies now support impoverished single mothers … replacing husbands with the state' (Wolf, 2013, 136), but it is bad policy to replace husbands with the state when it may be possible to intervene to prevent it. The proposal in this book is that the substitution stops. Known risks to children who are born to mothers and fathers on welfare should not be ignored.

The proposal, no contraception, no dole, is not a policy of eugenics. It is not the trait of the individual that is in play here; rather, it is the circumstances under which the person makes choices about their future. The aim is to prevent a woman from becoming pregnant at a time when her prospects for caring for a child are at a low ebb. Being on a benefit is a low ebb. When a woman, with the help of a benefit, re-establishes herself in a job or a family, she is free to make up her own mind about childbirth. As a consequence of the policy it may well be that the woman has fewer children and will be better placed to care for them, but that is her choice. In any event, the policy will act as a

---

37 Greg Melleuish, ' "Breeder's licence" a path to poorer society.' *The Australian* 14 January 2015.

strong incentive either not to take a benefit or to get off it as quickly as possible. It may also act as a brake on those men who wish to pressure a young woman to start a family when they do not wish.

For those who are interested in eugenic arguments I would strongly recommend they read the essay by Frank Salter, 'Eugenics, ready or not' (Salter, 2015). Salter reminds the reader that eugenics is a fact of everyday life. New *in vitro* fertilisation (IVF) techniques, for example, allow parents and doctors to avoid known medical risks to babies. Britain has recently approved the use of 'three-parent' IVF to remove defective mitochondrial DNA from babies. There is also a growing market for eugenics. For example, Monash IVF, with sales of $114 million, offers the latest technology for genetically screening embryos.

Human mating has eugenic implications. Marriage laws are eugenic to the extent that they guard against inbreeding. For example, marriages are void if 'the parties are within a prohibited relationship', which are marriages 'between a person and an ancestor or descendant of the person', or 'between a brother and a sister (whether of the whole blood or the half-blood)'. Interestingly, an adopted child is deemed to be 'the natural relationship of child and parent' (*Marriage Act* 1961 (Cth) s. 23).

In many ways, governments and custom specifically address eugenic questions: the current proposal does not. There is an important distinction that Salter makes, and is a good principle to follow. A eugenic outcome that follows from those who would normally have larger families having smaller families should not be held to be eugenic. Rather, judgments should be made on other criteria, such as the level of obligation that may be considered reasonable for a welfare recipient to fulfill, the degree of coercion involved, and the freedom to avoid the obligations.

Richard Lynn has considered proposals for comprehensive parental licensing programs. The essential feature of these schemes is that they require everyone to have a parental license to have children (Lynn, 2001, 2005). A major problem in formulating a parental licensing program is that it is difficult to devise an effective and practical way to prevent unlicensed couples from having children. Another is that the application would be very widespread, applying to the vast majority for whom a license would not be necessary. All such proposals adopt as their starting point the position that some couples are unfit to rear children. For example, it may be argued that couples who are psychopaths would tend to produce children who would become psychopaths (Lynn, 2001, 213). But why apply to all couples a very tough test to prevent a problem that may only arise among a tiny minority?

Civil liberties arguments are crucial in this debate, but they are not as cut and dried as some would have. The United Nations Declaration on Human Rights, which asserts that everyone has the right to have unlimited numbers of children, would prevent parental licensing plans. Nevertheless, there are indisputably some couples that neglect, ill-treat, abuse, and even kill their children. These people are plainly not fit to be parents, and the right to parenthood should not be extended to them. Australia clearly recognises this by having legal provisions and agencies to remove from their parents children who are ill-treated and to punish the parents. While it should be possible to establish in principle that some people are unfit to be parents and to deny them the parental license, the problem of preventing them from having children is formidable. Further, because Lynn is debating extreme cases, the benefits, if achievable because of compliance issues, are very small, and the impingement on liberties very large.

Nevertheless, law is invoked to remove children from parents to be adopted, fostered, or placed in institutions. But this is unlikely to make a significant contribution to preventing their birth, which is Lynn's concern, or to delaying their birth until such time as parents are better prepared, which is mine. Licensing and other allied eugenic proposals are not wise and not part of compulsory LARCs for those who choose a benefit.

Breaching human rights

There are rights associated with having children and there are rights associated with taking benefits. The right to bear children should be left untrammelled, unless, in the extreme case of risk to the mother and her inability to assess the situation, in which case, that right should be overridden. The case of DD in the United Kingdom (Court of Protection, 2015), discussed in chapter two, is one where the judge had a clear basis on which to rule that the mother be taken to hospital for sterilisation. The same, severely mentally incapacitated woman, however, had six previous children all of whom had been taken into care. They were highly likely to be low IQ, but that is not reason enough to prevent their birth. Neither could they be cared for, but that is not reason enough to prevent their birth.

While the mother was on a welfare benefit she should not have presumed that the state would stand in the stead of the father to care for them. The assumption that the child is the parent's responsibility was clearly breached in that case, at least six times over. Having someone sterilised for their own health is tough but sensible; allowing the birth of the six, knowing the risks, was heartless and foolish. The United Kingdom could invoke a principle that a child should not be born when the mother is on a benefit. The state should not stand in the place of a father nor substitute for the mother's responsibility to care for the child, where it is possible to intervene to prevent that occurring.

Wishing that the civil right to access welfare benefits is a human right does not make it so. Typically, human rights are very narrowly defined. The best explanation is that there are two forms of rights. Negative rights, the right to go about one's business free from interference, which includes guarantees that arise in liberal democracies such as free speech, assembly, to participate in elections and so on, are securable by law and cost little. Positive rights, however, rely on agreement for others to pay.

The United Nations Universal Declaration of Human Rights of 1948 included all the major welfare rights. For example, Article 25 states broadly that everyone has the right to a standard of living adequate for the health and well-being of himself and his family, including food, clothing, housing and medical care and necessary social services, and the right to social security in the event of unemployment, sickness, disability, widowhood, old age, or other lack of livelihood in circumstances beyond his control. Article 25 is a good example of how extensive – some would say lavish – proposed welfare rights have become.

The declaration also states in Article 29.1: 'Everyone has duties to the community …'. Indeed they do, because the so-called right to welfare arises in the context of an insurance system, where each agrees to make a contribution to the community in order to secure the right to draw on the benefit should it become necessary. These rights are conditional. For example, in a wild moment some assert that there is a right to employment in Australia. There is not and never has been. There is a right, granted to permanent residents, to unemployment benefit limited by an income and assets test. Access to benefits is also governed by obligations. For example, access to an unemployment benefit is granted on the assumption that the beneficiary will search for work, not to have children. Access to parenting payment is granted to care for existing children, not to have more children. Access to Austudy is granted to improve one's chances of gaining employment, not to stay out of the workforce to have children. Access to a disability support pension is granted because one is unable to make a contribution through the workforce. Having children while on that benefit undermines its essential purpose.

It is plain that welfare rights exist, in some parts of the world, as legal rights. The question, however, is what sort of grounds those rights have. Are they also ethical rights? Consider the argument that a human right is a claim of all humans, as humans, against all other humans. If there were a human right to welfare, it would therefore seem that everyone would have a claim to some unspecified minimum provision on every other individual. But few think that. Rather, it is clear that only members of a particular group, for example, citizens, can claim welfare from their government. This suggests that welfare rights are, at most, ethical rights held by citizens (Griffin, 2000, 30). The content of the right to welfare is determined, not by universal human status, but by particular social conditions. Those social conditions are determined within nations. Citizens within nations set the rules.

Many of the negative duties correlated with human rights (for example, not denying autonomy) themselves involve positive duties (for example, ensuring conditions for the exercise of autonomy). This line of thought, suggested by Griffin, suggests that human rights are protections of our human standing – that is, of our actually possessing it. 'Does that not mean that human rights include a right to welfare?' (Griffin, 2000, 43). Griffin argues that one must be able actually to exercise autonomy in order to exercise a human right and that denial of benefits would deny that exercise. Even on this generous interpretation, what does delaying having a child do for exercising autonomy? Indeed, it may enhance it. Actually possessing the right to welfare depends on the circumstances of the nation and, in a democratic nation, the agreement of a majority of citizens. Welfare rights are no more than the stuff of politics, agreement to pay each other when and if things go wrong. If Australians want to enforce rules on beneficiaries, when beneficiaries have a choice not to take welfare, then these obligations hardly undermine their human rights.

Blaming the victim merry-go-round

The most difficult part of the blaming the victim critique is to know who else to blame. For instance, there is a strong body of opinion that poverty is at the heart of intergenerational welfare dependence and that neither culture nor welfare plays a part. But where neither culture nor welfare play a part it is difficult to know how much money it takes to make people not poor. Those who blame society usually have no solutions for the poor.

Daniel Patrick Moynihan was a long-standing United States Democrat Senator and a brilliant intellectual. In 1965, as an Assistant Secretary of Labor, a public servant, Moynihan wrote the report *The Negro Family: the case for national action*. He eschewed cultural explanations for the collapse of the black family and placed blame on the legacy of slavery and economic discrimination that left black men unable to provide for their own. Moynihan's solution, which was largely lost in the controversy the report generated, was 'to bring the structure of the Negro family in line with the rest of our society' by providing work for black men. To provide that work, Moynihan called for both racial quotas and European-style family allowances. In United States political terms, the proposals were very radical.

President L. B. Johnson initiated a War on Poverty, which took up some of Moynihan's proposals but, unfortunately, and largely because of a misreading of the report by critics, the War on Poverty and Moynihan's report were characterised as a war on the poor, especially the black urban poor. Since that time, any proposals that appear to want to change the circumstances and behaviour of the poor, other than give them money, have been blocked by the use of the allegation blaming the poor. The result has been timidity in public policy.

American authors, Carbone and Cahn, suggest that Moynihan's explanation, that the loss of jobs for the urban black changed family structure in black families, ran into trouble when the same explanation was not used to explain changes in white families. He attributed many of the 'pathologies' of the black family to the matriarchy of women who had to step in to fill the breach left by men. In the rush to defend the black families larger issues were missed. Reworking this debate is fertile ground for the LARCs proposal. Carbone and Cahn argue that, for example, while unemployment is a cause of family strife, other factors, in particular, women's attitudes to partnering, men's attitudes to partnering and the freedom to have or not to have sex and children in any circumstances, played a part. Culture and mores changed, not simply economies. Some groups have been more susceptible to change than others.

Carbone and Cahn pose the question, how does a loss of employment change cultural norms, and how does gender affect the result (Carbone, 2014, 27)? Their answers are that the freedom of women to choose partners changed because they could work and/or be assisted by government, because the mores of sex changed, because marriage and partnership changed, and protection from pregnancy changed. This characterisation strikes me as true and accurate for Australia. By contrast, Charles Murray, *Coming Apart: the state of white America* (Murray, 2013), argues that success reflects intelligence and is therefore difficult for the government to change. Carbone and Cahn's critique of Murray is that he ignores the loss of good jobs for working class men and improved employment prospects for women. Instead, he concentrated on the morals of the poor.

Murray commences his analysis by tracing a string of cultural changes in the United States from which Murray's vision of America changed forever and, for many Americans, for the worse. Murray argued that the United States lost its unique civic culture, a 'civil religion'. 'To be American was to be different from other nationalities ... that culture is unravelling.' He was referring to class division, specifically the emergence of an educated elite and a poorly educated lower class and that there was little in common between the two (Murray, 2013, 12). He describes a situation in the United States where merit rules and only the most intelligent attend elite schools and intermarry, thus reinforcing the meritocracy. 'The reason that upper-middle-class children dominate the population of elite schools is that the parents of the upper middle-class now produce a disproportionate number of the smartest children, in a world based on a close relationship between brains and reward, reinforcing the elite' (Murray, 2013, 60).

Murray provides abundant evidence that among white males especially there has been a decline in 'industriousness', for example, an 'unbelievable' rise in physical disability when work is becoming physically less risky and demanding, a decline in marriage, a rise in divorce and the number of children affected by divorce and born outside of marriage, and a decline in religiosity. There is little dissent of his observations, but he argues 'a social democrat may see a compelling case for the redistribution of wealth. A social conservative may see a compelling case for government policies that support marriage, religion and traditional values.' Murray is a libertarian and sees 'a compelling case for returning to the founders' conception of limited government' (Murray, 2013, 238). Murray decries the

'Europe syndrome', 'that the purpose of life is to while away the time between birth and death as pleasantly as possible, and the purpose of government is to make it as easy as possible to while away the time as pleasantly as possible' (Murray, 2013, 287).

Murray rails against the new elite which has abdicated its responsibility to 'set and promulgate' standards of behaviour. He rails against the European welfare state, among other reasons for its 'looming bankruptcy' and its encouragement to give up on work. With these, I agree. I do not agree with Murray, however, that the welfare state caused the breakdown of the family. I believe that the women's revolution caused the breakdown of the 'traditional' family and that it was right and inevitable. However, the family is and will make a comeback as men and women renegotiate their respective roles within the partnership of marriage. His solutions to poverty and intergenerational welfare dependence, which are to encourage hard work, marriage and religion, may help, but how does one do this? How does this antidote to his loss of American 'civil religion' stop the formation of families without fathers? Nor do I agree with Carbone and Cahn who blame the breakdown on family at the lower end on inequality, especially loss of jobs, or job stability. In Australia, unemployment has been low for a long time, inequality is not pronounced and, in any event, there are more transfers going on than was the case when the family started to come apart.

What Carbone and Cahn offer though is a very good question: 'if the shotgun wedding is dead as a response to pregnancy, why does anyone get married without the threat?' (Carbone, 2014, 36). As they argue, how did middle class women persuade a man to marry them without getting pregnant, and why do less well educated women having children at younger ages become more critical of partners on offer to them? The argument is that, shortly after the pill became available, educated women began to delay marriage earlier, and to a greater degree, than less-educated women. The more educated are more likely to marry, which was not always the case. University graduates of an earlier period, of whom there were admittedly few, were less likely than others to marry. At the same time, male graduates delayed marriage. Graduate women had a bigger choice of graduates than was otherwise the case: 'a thicker market'. Graduates found each other. 'The leaders of the sexual revolution reaped its benefits and found their way back into traditional family life' (Carbone, 2014, 41). Women have incomes and are less reliant on men; they expect more of men. Carbone and Cahn also argue that economies have become unfair, creating more bad jobs and fewer good ones. A consequence is a shortage of eligible men at the lower end.

Quoting two 'poverty' researchers, 'young disadvantaged couples who have children together may emerge from the euphoria of the delivery room only to find they have astoundingly little in common' (Carbone, 2014, 97). As they go on to say,

> *the same may have been true of couples in the sixties, but the difference is that they were married by the time they got to the delivery room and embedded in a family system that made divorce hard ... In those days the husband could get a job that paid substantially more than the wife ... , and her financial dependence gave her little choice but to defer to the authority that his income and his gender conferred on him.* (Carbone, 2014, 97)

Carbone and Cahn's (and Murray's) acute observations of marriage markets and changed mores fail to provide satisfactory policy solutions. The first wants an economic revolution, the second wants a moral revolution. Neither revolution is about to happen, or not in the way they wish, and is probably highly inadvisable. Missing are observations about why poor people act as they do, often acting as their own worst enemy. It is not blaming the poor to observe that the poor may make bad judgments. The behavioural economist, Sendhil Mullainathan of Harvard University, and psychologist Eldar Shafir of Princeton University attribute an extraordinary range of societal problems among the rich and poor, to scarcity. Not to the attributes of the person, but to the context of the scarcity under which they operate. As they explain, scarcity raises the cost of error because it operates like a tax; it provides more opportunity to make misguided choices because many operate with a very narrow or tunnel vision.

Choices based on a focus on the immediate future and made under taxing conditions can be disastrous.

One of scores of examples provided by the authors suffices for our purposes. They cite research that diabetics take their medication only 50 to 70 per cent of the time. Brilliant pharmacology comes to nought because someone forgot to take their tablet. 'The poor take their medication least consistently'. In another case, the poor are worse parents. They are harsher with their children, less consistent, more disconnected and thus 'appear less loving. They are more likely to take out their own anger on the child'. Especially important in the context of the proposal, 'poor women are less likely to eat properly or engage in prenatal care' (regardless of availability of food and medicine). Moreover, the 'poor in the United States who are on Medicaid pay nothing for their medications, yet they fail to take them regularly' (Mullainathan, 2015, 151).

Their startling conclusion is that just as failure causes poverty, poverty causes failure. Many public health programs rely on the poor to absorb new information. Campaigns try to educate the public about the importance of eating healthier, smoking less, obtaining prenatal care and so on. So much of these changes require individual discipline and self-control which the poor may not have. This is not a moral observation from the researchers, rather it is an observation of people who are, literally, taxed by their circumstances such that they lack the foresight to make sound judgements in their best interest. The big message from this research is that rewards and penalties for the poor and the programs on offer to help need to be focussed on immediate needs and behaviours, not the long-term needs that require planning and foresight. Cashless cards for some welfare recipients in Australia are an experiment that appears to be based on this thinking.

Policy to tackle intergenerational welfare dependence should aim to change behaviour and it should be effective. Fixing intergenerational welfare is difficult but replaying the same interventions is not helpful. For example, women with higher levels of educational qualification tend to have fewer children than do those with lower education levels (ABS, 2008, 5). Is the correct intervention to educate the poor or have them have fewer children? The relationship between class and educational outcomes persists, despite generations of compulsory, heavily-funded public education. Some people just do not learn. Education has been free for generations, but cultures persist. The reasons may be insuperable, but the interventions that may assist need to be immediate and consequential.

While to intervene less in a person's life has its hazards, to intervene more in a person's life also has its hazards. To intervene with a different purpose has a chance. Class or welfare is not destiny. People from poor backgrounds succeed all of the time. The issue is about shortening the odds on success among those most likely to fail. Explaining why the poor make poor choices is not to blame the poor; rather, it provides insight into how poor choices can be harmful. Having a child while on a benefit is a poor choice.

Stigmatising – not at all

The risk that a group of people may be stigmatised by the policy of compulsory LARCs is real. For example, because some teenage mothers fail as mothers, it would be wrong to cast a pall over all teenage mothers. A large study of teenage mothers undertaken at South Brisbane confirms that 'teenage pregnancy is a phenomenon of poverty and possibly low intelligence' but, as the authors caution, 'not all teenage mothers and their offspring have adverse outcomes, and that many if not the majority have good outcomes.' Fourteen per cent of the offspring of teenage mothers in the study were delinquent compared to eight per cent of the offspring of older mothers, which suggested 86 per cent of the offspring of teenage mothers were not delinquent. The authors concluded that to 'focus on the negative outcomes for young parents run(s) the risk of stigmatising all such parents and their offspring' (Shaw, 2006, 2537).

It is true that parents feel the pressure of community expectation. Another Australian study of 48 parents parenting alone who were on social security payments found that parents described a range of negative experiences, including how they needed to prove their entitlement to help repeatedly, leaving them feel as if they were undeserving.

One parent described her experience in buying a rail ticket with her concession card:

> *There's an extremely rude man that works there (Rail Company) and I went in there and paid for a ticket one day and he turned around and said to me "your concession card our tax money pays for that". So I wasn't too impressed to hear that.*

One mother was incensed when she felt judged by services:

> *Yeah, they don't know me from a bar of soap and I don't think they have the right to judge me and they don't know that I've been working since I was 15 till 6 weeks before I had my baby I hadn't stopped working, and I can't help I'm a single mum. But they didn't have the right to judge me.*

One mother whose 12-year-old son had suffered a heart attack said:

> *I just feel like I had to leave my job because my son was ill. And you know they (Centrelink) are very pushy about you getting back into the work force ... you know we've had a harrowing year and I know they want me to go back into the work force, but ... I still just want to spend a little bit more time with my son.*

> *I have three kids, I've always been out there trying to give back to the community but at the moment it's been sort of when I need the help I can't get it, to better myself, to get back into the workforce, I just can't get it.* (McArthur, 2013, 163)

Another Australian study, based on 35 young parents in 2010 in NSW and NT, and two focus groups with 14 young mothers in Canberra, made similar pleas (McArthur, 2013). The study suggests that policy and service responses that further stigmatise younger mothers risk undermining their willingness to engage with the formal and informal support systems that could otherwise assist them. Responses that appear least helpful to younger mothers and their children are those that identify them as requiring extra help because of weaknesses in their parenting, simply by virtue of their age and income. Instead, consideration should focus on how to provide 'tailored support and encouragement'. The authors concluded that the group of younger mothers did not regard themselves as 'jobless' or 'aimless' on welfare and almost all looked forward with high expectations to 'relinquishing reliance on income support as soon as' they could (McArthur & Winkworth, 2013, 60).

The problem is not that young mothers may be under pressure but how this may be prevented in order to save them from such a life. It is a strange argument to suggest that having placed themselves in a position where they find life difficult, by becoming pregnant, fellow citizens should pay for all their dreams to become educated and raise a family, which they may have achieved by their own means had they been assisted to plan their life. Without that assistance, for example, where a partner leaves a mother to fend for herself, or himself, of course support should be readily available. While there is a risk, the risk of stigmatising teenage mothers is not so great when all women on a benefit are the subjects of the policy. Those on a benefit subject to the policy may be stigmatised, but that risk pales in comparison to those known risks of intergenerational dependence.

Population control – wrong camp

No contraception, no dole has received support from the population control advocates. Thanks, but no thanks. For a start, as figure 4.1 shows, fertility rates in Australia crashed in the 1970s at the introduction of the pill and for all of the reasons discussed in chapter four. In any event, the object of the exercise is not to have fewer babies, but that women plan to have them in circumstances when they can afford them and where there is a supportive partner.

Besides, not only does Australia's contribution to world population growth barely register, there is good evidence that, were it possible, a major depression in fertility world-wide would make little difference to, for example, resource depletion in the near and medium term.

Eco-fatalists have argued that the planet's 'large, growing, and over-consuming human population, especially the increasing affluent component, is rapidly eroding many of the Earth's natural ecosystems'. They pose the question, if 'society were to encourage lower per capita fertility, how long might fertility reduction take to make a meaningful impact?' In a recent study of global human population change to the year 2100, a plausible range of outcomes was generated by adjusting various fertility and mortality rates involving long- and short-term interventions. The study concluded that, 'even one-child policies imposed worldwide and catastrophic mortality events would still likely result in 5-10 billion people by 2100' (Bradshaw, 2014, 16610). Demographic momentum alone ensures that there are no easy ways to change the broad trends of human population size this century.

The LARC proposal in Australia, which would have minimal impact on fertility overall, cannot be counted among the prime candidates for the over-population toolkit.

7

Opening debate

Intergenerational welfare dependence is real

Intergenerational welfare dependence is real. Mothers with the most economic independence and best educated are leading the way in establishing stable unions based on a more equal sharing of parental responsibilities. Mothers with poor education or just poor are finding single motherhood without stable relationships. There is, to some extent, a 'divergence of destinies' occurring in the aftermath of the second demographic transition (McLanahan, 2004, 623).

But is it enough to provide greater resources to the poor? Early intervention is the great hope of policy-makers in recent times, but it is an admission that, unless a child has a different upbringing than the one it is likely to receive in some households then the chances of its leading a fulfilling life is diminished. There are scores of programs that attempt to help, mostly, tidy up after the damage is done.

The proposition in this book is that the first line of intervention should be to prevent the birth of a child to a parent who is not ready to care for the child. This is early intervention. The trigger is the parent seeking a benefit from the taxpayer. Delaying having a child until the parent or parents are ready, that is, are employed and established in a relationship is standard practice for most couples. Alas, for others it is not. Those couples or, indeed, individuals can be led astray by the inducement of payments to parents for the very fact of producing a child. The retort, 'could you live on the dole?', may well be thrown at the proposition that anyone would have a child to receive a miserly benefit is not a defence against the risk that any incentive to not plan for a child is a bad incentive. Knowing that some support is available may tilt the balance towards pregnancy.

There are two pieces of information essential to open debate on the no contraception, no dole proposal: how many may be affected and which method is most likely to be effective in the take up of LARCs. As to the latter, it will be essential to experiment and trial different approaches. Fortunately, trials have been a central part of social security policy for its entire history, indeed, the introduction of the age pension was remarked upon at the time as an experiment. A contemporaneous comment on the *Invalid and Old-Age Pensions Act* 1908 suggested, 'This law must be regarded as a social experiment, the success or otherwise of which has yet to be shown by experience' (Herscovitch, 2008, 51).

Baby Bonus experiment

Politicians are never slow to spend money to buy votes, but sometimes they fail to anticipate the consequences. In 2004, the Australian Government introduced the offer of a cash payment of $3,000 to all women on the birth of a new baby. The baby bonus was increased to $4,000 in 2006 and to $5,000 in 2008. The politicians said that the bonus was designed to boost the fertility rate. It was true that Australia was experiencing the lowest fertility trends in its history but, as we know from figure 4.1, the fertility rate had tanked thirty years earlier and remained low. At the height of the resources boom, with taxation revenue flowing into Treasury coffers, the reason for the baby bonus was no more, and no less, than that there was money to burn.

There have been strong denials from the framers of the baby bonus that any woman or family would have a child because of the bonus. A recent case suggests otherwise. During their relationship, the parties to the case had seven children. The parties both travelled to Lebanon with the four children of the marriage who had been born at that time. They returned to Australia several months later, leaving one child in Lebanon. The mother returned to Lebanon and then returned to Australia leaving three children in Lebanon. The mother claimed that she returned to Australia only after being told by the father that her Centrelink benefits were going to be stopped, and she needed to return to Australia to renew them. In 2011, the mother went back to Lebanon with two children only. In 2012, the mother returned to Australia with one child. The mother claimed that she returned to Australia at the behest of the father, to enable their seventh child to be born in Australia and to collect the baby bonus (Family Court of Australia (a), 2014).

Another case reveals that in tormented lives incentives can play a part in bad decisions. The application was for the care and protection of children aged six, four, and two years. There was substantial environmental neglect in an old Ministry of Housing flat, and the oldest child was on occasions found wandering some distance from home. The parents had disappeared from the family home. The department removed the three older children and gave them to the paternal grandmother and her friend.

The mother had two older children, one 12 years, was adopted at birth and the mother had not seen him since. The second, 11 years, was the subject of a permanent care order and was in the care of the maternal grandmother and her friend. One child had resided since he was four days old with the children's maternal uncle and his wife.

The father had eight siblings. His father was an alcoholic. The father's mother was a chronic gambler. His parents separated when he was 11 years old owing to continuous arguments and domestic violence. The mother said that she just 'shut down' when her parents separated due to continuous conflict when she was 11 years old. The maternal grandmother regrets not having been a better mother to the mother but was controlled so much by her husband at that time and did not dare cross him.

Counsel for the mother said she had been instructed to ask the magistrate if he would be able to order that her client be paid the baby bonus for one of the children which she was instructed, had been paid to carers (Children's Court of Victoria, 2008).

Between 2001 and 2008 Australia's total fertility rate increased from 1.73 to 1.96 but, according to one study, the effect of the baby bonus was 'not significantly different from zero'. It was a time of economic boom and real incomes had increased, people felt confident to start a family or increase the one they had (Parr, 2011, 228). In other words, at best, the baby bonus was a waste of money. The baby bonus experiment failed and was quietly withdrawn, but not without leaving a painful legacy.

Other studies suggest that it was not simply the boom, but the bonus that caused an increase in fertility. One estimate was that about 108,000 babies were born because of the inducement attributable to the bonus and that the cost per extra child, for example in health care costs and other payments, was $43,000 (Sinclair, 2012, 78). Worse still, the bonus may have provided an incentive for women to leave the workforce or remain outside it. The greatest increase in the birth rate in NSW, relative to the trend, was observed in teenagers.[38] A second study estimated that the bonus 'exerted a small though positive and significant effect on fertility' and that 'low-income women are more responsive to cash payments.' Further, the marginal cost per additional child figure was at least $126,000. 'This cost estimate is sufficiently high that policy-makers may wish to reconsider cash benefits relative to alternative policies if enhancing fertility is the only goal' (Drago, 2011, 394).

A further analysis suggested that the baby bonus also had the potential to 'drain labour supply' by encouraging increased childbearing without offering any incentive for women to maintain or strengthen their workforce involvement. When combined with other maternity-related benefits such as the Family Tax Benefit Part B, the baby bonus did more to reward women for staying out of the workforce than to promote their workforce participation. The baby bonus policy had the strongest incentive effect on women from lower-income households because lower-income households are likely to be more reliant on welfare to assist with the costs of raising a family. The bottom line

---

38 In Western Australia the greatest increase in births was among those women living in high socio-economic areas, but this does not prove that those were not poor or very young (Sinclair, 2012, 86).

was that 'the baby bonus may well have had the effect of exacerbating welfare dependency' (Risse, 2010, 231).

The following is an extract from a letter to a member of federal Parliament, 2012.

> *As a Home-Start Parenting Co-ordinator I work with mums and dads with children under the age of 8 years, running parenting courses for parents ...*
>
> *I feel that I am working with a lost generation of parents, many of whom experienced very difficult childhoods and were not parented very well themselves.*
>
> *I don't believe it is rocket science that if the Baby Bonus was attached to parenting programs things would change for the better ... Perhaps then we would not see so many of our parents failing and their children taken into care.*[39]

Others were left to deal with the outcomes of pregnancies that, but for the baby bonus, may not have occurred. The letter from a social worker to a local federal member of Parliament tells a sad tale. The baby bonus experiment probably resulted in tens of thousands of unplanned births and may have exacerbated welfare dependency. Spending a little to delay and possibly prevent such births seems like a good investment by comparison.

What is the purpose of social security?

The architects of the baby bonus failed to consider the consequences of their actions and probably took no notice of the purpose for which the social security system had been established. A recent major report on welfare to the Minister for Social Services had quite a lot to say about the purpose of social security. Here are three themes prominent in the report:

- *Supporting people to live a life they value should be a core value of the social support system.*

---

39 The letter was made available to the author on promise of anonymity, June 2015.

- *People who can work should work.*

- *A system should be underpinned by mutual obligations that ensure the provision of support is matched by individual responsibility to develop personal capability.* (Reference Group, 2015)

The first theme, supporting people to live a life they value, is a noble sentiment, but what if the values held by a welfare recipient clash with the second theme, that people who can work should work? For example, what if a woman, or a man, values having a child above all else? Should taxpayers support a person or a couple having a child when individuals are free to do so without intervention? Being free to pursue the value of having children really means being free to earn an income to raise children. The need to support one's own desires seems to be forgotten in the world of social security aspiration and compassionate welfarism.

While there are many who require social security permanently, all others should move off benefit as soon as possible. At the very least, having a child while on a benefit delays coming off benefit, and it may be a sure way to remain on benefits. It is not a responsible act. To have a child while on a benefit reverses the assumption under which all Australians live and which social security assumes, that is, to make every effort to look after oneself and one's family.

The third theme is that the taxpayer should require something in return for the benefit granted to a recipient; in other words, there must be mutual obligation. The crux of mutual obligation is the recipient should prepare for work, not motherhood. Motherhood requires the support of a partner, not taxpayers, in a continuing relationship. Enrolling in training and education in order to secure a job and an income to support a child is an acceptable path. Going straight on benefits to have a child is not.

Mutual obligation

Requiring recipients to perform various tasks is not a form of blaming the poor because without mutual obligations the chances of remaining poor increase. The reasons why people make bad decisions, such as having babies when on a benefit, may be rational. Their outlook may be so focussed on their desire to fulfil a role, or simply because there is an incentive attached, that taking the benefit is rational. But if the decision is likely to be harmful and can be prevented at no great cost to the recipient, then contraception should be part of the contract.

The extent of obligations imposed on beneficiaries has, in recent years, expanded enormously. For example, in New Zealand, welfare beneficiaries are subject to drug tests. The view is that, consistent with the New Zealand Bill of Rights, individuals receiving welfare should have the right to refuse to undertake drug or alcohol treatment but the right to refuse treatment does not extend to continuing to receive welfare if the refusal means a person is then unavailable for work (Rebstock, 2011, 76).

The former Prime Minister, Tony Abbott, and Scott Morrison, then Minister for Social Services, recently announced a 'No jab', 'no pay' policy, which indicated a further step along the path to mutual obligations. The Government will end the conscientious objector exemption on children's vaccination for access to taxpayer-funded Child Care Benefits, the Child Care Rebate and the Family Tax Benefit Part A by end of year supplement from 1 January 2016. Existing exemptions on medical or religious grounds will continue. An objection on religious grounds will only be available where the person is affiliated with a religious group where the governing body has a formally registered objection approved by the Government. This means that vaccine objectors will not be able to access these government payments. More than 39,000 children less than seven years of age are not vaccinated because their parents are vaccine objectors. The Government argued that the 'choice made by families not to immunise their children is not supported by public policy or medical research nor should such action be supported by taxpayers in the form of child care payments.'[40]

The income management scheme which, as chapter five explained, directs a proportion of a person's income support and family assistance payments to the purchase of food, clothing and rent makes it absolutely clear that it is not acceptable to smoke, drink and gamble taxpayer's money. In addition to the direct obligation on the recipient, however, it is also abundantly clear that, for example, children of recipients should attend school. Some argue, quite validly, that the latter type of obligation is 'ill-placed' and has unsettled the balance in welfare law between 'pointing welfare recipients in the direction of the good, common life, and directing them in exactly how to live such a life' (Stephens, 2013, 398).

It would be harsh if a benefit to the whole society were gained at a cost to the individual beneficiary. If, however, there is a direct benefit, or at least no harm to the individual concerned and the coercion is neither burdensome nor permanent, intervention may be warranted. There is an anticipatory element to new obligations around the behaviour of the children of beneficiaries precisely because there is now hard evidence of intergenerational dependence on welfare. It is no longer possible to ignore the evidence and so interventions that seek to stop the intergenerational cycle are worth exploring despite the risk of the state directing recipients how to live a life they value.

Feasible candidates

The chances of implementing the policy of 'no contraception, no dole' would improve if the obligations can be confined to those who would benefit most. The recent report to the Minister for Social Services had two important points to make about focussing attention and early intervention.

The new social support system should identify and invest in the groups at greatest risk of remaining on income support long term,

---

40 Department of Human Services, 'Immunising your children', www.humanservices. gov.au accessed 9 July 2015.

with a capacity for self reliance.

The social support system is failing to identify groups at risk of long term income support dependence and needs to refocus on early intervention and support through difficult transitions. (Reference Group, 2015).

The report sang the praises of an 'investment approach' to reduce future liability associated with long-term income support dependence by targeting investment to build people's self-reliance. New Zealand has introduced an investment approach for the long-term management of its income support system. This strategy is focused on getting people into jobs through investment in evidence-based services where return on investment is likely to be highest. A key aspect of this approach is the use of an actuarial valuation to establish lifetime costs (liability) of both the overall income support system and of specific groups within the system. This appears obvious in that the longer a person stays on benefit, and the deeper and more extensive their problems, the more is the cost of keeping them. Theoretically, the earlier the intervention, the greater the amount saved.

Controlling fertility among those dependent on welfare would seem to be very strong candidate for the investment approach. Women who choose to have a child while on benefit are converts from self-reliance to dependence. Women of fertile age who are otherwise well are almost certainly a good investment in self-reliance. The extra cost in preventing pregnancy is minimal. The life-long return on a planned pregnancy may be substantial. In New Zealand, an estimated one in seven sole parents (and ultimately one in four of current sole parent beneficiaries) who enter the benefit system will have an additional child while on a benefit (Rebstock, 2011, 76). In 2010, 4,800 newborns (7.5 per cent of all live births) were included in the benefit of an existing Domestic Purposes Benefit client. The on-benefit rate has risen since 1997, from under 35 births per 1,000 women receiving DPB-Sole Parent in 1997 to over 50 births per 1,000 women receiving DPB-SP in 2010 (NZ Ministry for Social Development (c), 2012, 2).

How many in Australia?

In Australia, we now know that there are perhaps as many as 60,000 children born each year to women who are on a benefit. There are slightly more than 300,000 births in Australia per year, so almost 20 per cent are born to a woman on a benefit (ABS (b), 2014). A feasible no contraception, no dole policy must be targeted to the people most likely to benefit. There are some benefits where the number of beneficiaries who have given birth is very low in absolute, or in relative, terms to those in the category of benefit. The return to the intervention among that class of beneficiary is therefore low.

Table 7.1 Children born in calendar year 2014 in the care of female beneficiaries

Type of benefit	Children born in 2014 in the care of a female recipient in the month prior to the birth	Children born in 2014 in the care of a female recipient at birth
Austudy	342	236
Carer payment	2,802	2,826
Disability support pension	2,969	3,016
Newstart allowance	11,469	6,216
Parenting payment partnered	12,831	18,271
Parenting payment single	20,711	30,542
Youth allowance (apprentice)	24	8
Youth allowance (other)	6,652	2,410
Youth allowance (student)	1,029	425

Source: Department of Social Security, private correspondence, 2015

The number of children in the care of women on various benefits, calculated at two different times is set out in table 7.1. By comparing these numbers with those numbers of beneficiaries published by the Department of Social Services, *Income support customers: a statistical overview* (Department of Social Services, 2014) it is possible to narrow the field of likely candidates for the policy.

Austudy

Austudy is a means-tested, fortnightly payment for individuals aged 25 years and over who are either undertaking full-time qualifying study in an approved course at an approved educational institution; or undertaking a full-time Australian Apprenticeship. There were 35,000 women age 25-39 receiving Austudy in 2013.

Abstudy is a means-tested living allowance and a range of supplementary benefits for Aboriginal and Torres Strait Islander full-time students and apprentices. Some supplementary benefits are available to part-time students. There were 8,000 women age 20 or older receiving Abstudy in 2013. Given that there are only between 342 and 236 women who may have given birth to child while on Austudy it would be a poor return for effort to target this group of beneficiaries.

Carer payment

Carer payment is for carers who provide constant care in the home of the person(s) being cared for, and who, because of the demands of their caring role, are unable to support themselves by participating substantially in the workforce. There were 45,000 women age 20-39 receiving carer payment in 2013. Carer Allowance is an income supplement available to people who provide daily care and attention for adults or children with disability or a severe medical condition, or who are frail aged. There were 108,000 women age 20-39 receiving carer allowance in 2013. Given that there are only between 2,802 and 2,826 women who may have given birth to child while on carer payment it may be a poor return for effort to target this group of beneficiaries.

Disability support pension

The number of women on a disability support pension has more than tripled in the period 1993-2013, from 115,00 to 381,000. In the same period the number of men on benefit increased from 291,000 to 441,000. The number of women aged 20-39 on a disability support pension in 2013 was 270,000. About 25 per cent of disability support pensioners are not permanent and remain on benefit for fewer than five years. Long-term pensioners appear to be older and remain until they shift to the age pension. Given that there are only between 2,969 and 3,016 women who may have given birth to child while on a disability pension it may be a poor return for effort to target this group of beneficiaries.

Newstart allowance

Newstart allowance is available to people aged 22 years or older and under the qualifying age for the age pension who are unemployed, or treated as unemployed and are looking for work, or participating in approved activities. There were 305,000 women age 21-39 receiving Newstart allowance in 2013. There are between 11,469 and 6,216 women who may have given birth to a child while on Newstart allowance, which make these beneficiaries candidates for consideration.

Parenting payment

Parenting payment was introduced to help people with children, particularly low-income families, by providing an independent income. Parenting payment is available to people with sole or primary responsibility for the care of a child and is payable to both single and partnered parents. Those on PP may be on other allowances or have a low income and be working, so this group is not to be added to the others, but perhaps provides a clearer picture of the probable target group.

The number on PP (single) has declined considerably since the high point of 416,000 women (of any age) in 2005 to 243,000 in 2013. There were 214,000 women up to age 39 receiving parenting payment (single) in 2013. Parenting payment (Partnered) is payable to only one member of a couple. To qualify for parenting payment (Partnered), partnered parents must have principal care of a child or children under the age of six years.

The numbers on PP (partnered) has declined considerably since the high point of 150,00 women (of any age) in 2005 to 94,000 in 2013. Changes to the payment in 2006 required beneficiaries to seek part-time work of at least 15 hours per week once their youngest child reaches the age of six years. They would be able to continue to receive payment until their youngest child reaches the age of sixteen years.[41] There were 88,000 women up to age 39 receiving PP (partnered) in 2013. There are between 33,542 and 48,813 women who may have given birth to a child while on a parenting payment, which make these beneficiaries candidates for consideration.

Youth allowance

Youth allowance (student and other) is for young people less than 22 years who are temporarily incapacitated or unemployed and looking for work. Family assistance payments are the primary form of government support for dependent full-time secondary students aged 16-19 years who live at home, until they finish school. Youth allowance then provides continuing support to young people as they finish school and progress to further education and training. There were 142,000 women age 20 or older receiving youth allowance in 2013. There are between 7,705 and 2,843 women who may have given birth to a child while on a youth allowance, which may make these beneficiaries candidates for consideration.

---

41 Employment and Workplace Relations Legislation Amendment (Welfare to Work and Other Measures) Bill 2005, Bills Digest no. 70 2005-06.

Poor compliance candidates

On the basis of the potential number of children born to women on a parenting payment, Newstart or a youth allowance these are the most likely candidates for the no contraception, no dole policy. A further refinement is to assess those who presently fail to comply with benefit obligations, including those on income management, as reported in chapter five.

As at December 2014 there were almost 900,000 job seekers in Australia engaged with their employment service providers, that is, on benefits. About 330,000 have been reported for non-compliance, either through a Participation Report or Non-Attendance Report, on one or multiple occasions. About 70,000 had five or more reports. There were 65,000 Participation Failures in the period October-December 2014. Participation Failures are applied where the Department of Human Services has assessed a Participation Report and has determined that the job seeker did not have a reasonable excuse. There were 270,000 income support payment suspensions in the period.

There were 116,000 with a 'vulnerability indicator', meaning that a job seeker has a diagnosed condition or personal circumstance (e.g. homelessness, mental illness) that may currently affect their capacity to comply with mutual obligation requirements, although it does not exempt a job seeker from these requirements (Department of Employment, 2014, 3). As at 30 September 2014, there were 39,984 cases where the paying parent was being managed by Intensive Collection Services of the Department of Human Services (HoR Standing Committee, 2015, 4.114).

The no contraception, no dole policy is an attempt to place a woman in a position where she can plan for a family, that is, to mimic the behaviour of a working couple that plan for a child. The policy should not be regarded as a punishment, which is the only reluctance that may apply to including in the policy purview those on the participation failure or vulnerability lists. However, such people are precisely those who are at risk of unsupported pregnancy.

What interventions work?

Strong compliance measures do not have a one hundred per cent success rate; no program is likely to have such a rate. Nevertheless, policy should aim for the highest compliance at least cost to both the client and the taxpayer. For some people the idea that it is not appropriate to have a child, or further children, while receiving welfare is a significant change in expectation and will require a very different pattern of welfare use. There are mixed results in programs where LARCs are free but not compulsory and there are mixed results in programs of other types, for example, employment, where compulsion and penalties fail in some cases. The incentives may work for some and not others. A study in 2012 involving Aboriginal students in Queensland schools, for example, found that 'in-kind' incentives for Aboriginal children to attend school were only effective for children in intact families (Dulleck, 2014).

Any policy must also be aware of incentives already in the system. An example is a day care that commenced to impose fines on parents who were late picking up their children. The assumption was that imposing a fine would act as an incentive to pick up the child on time. In fact, the reverse occurred. For the first time, parents knew the cost of late arrivals and were often prepared to pay the price. The previous incentives were unknown, but were implicit. They were things like respect for managers of the centre and imposition on staff time. The implicit incentives were displaced by the explicit disincentive and the net result was reduced compliance (Gneezy, 2013, 19).

It is not as if governments have not tried to reach people. A recent evaluation of three programs of the Stronger Families and Communities Strategy 2004-2009 for the Department of Families, Housing, Community Services and Indigenous Affairs questioned how and how effectively services engaged hard-to-reach populations (Cortis, 2009, v). The study identified indigenous families as the most hard-to-reach group, along with young parents and fathers.

Participant responses showed that defining which groups are considered hard-to-reach depended on the context. Community context is especially important. In non-metropolitan settings, for example, isolated families and those with transport difficulties were identified as particularly hard-to-reach. Staffing resources and context also matter, with the presence of a liaison officer or outreach worker helping to ensure that the intervention was able to engage with target populations (Cortis, 2009, vi). As one would expect from public program evaluations, in the face of failure the answer was for 'more sustainable funding arrangements to minimise disruption to relationship building processes, promote staffing stability, and support specialist outreach workers' (Cortis, 2009, vii). In other words, give them more money until they get it right.

The free LARCs scheme to beneficiary women and their daughters in New Zealand is in its early days, but here, too, it is clear that uptake is low. While most contraceptives are fully subsidised, the cost of doctor visits can be a barrier. Both Family Planning and primary care doctors normally charge for insertion of long acting reversible devices. The New Zealand initiative provided greater access for women beneficiaries to get professional medical advice on these contraceptives if they chose to. Along with New Zealand, the countries with the highest rates of sole parenthood and welfare receipt among sole parents are the United States and the United Kingdom. In the former case, financial disincentives are used as a measure to reduce non-marital pregnancies. In the United Kingdom the approach has been to focus on education and health services for sole parents, especially teenage parents. An early assessment of the New Zealand scheme's effectiveness found that only 35 women took up the Government's offer of free long-term contraception for beneficiaries in the first five months, far short of the number expected.[42]

There are examples elsewhere of greater success. Contraceptive CHOICE Project was a study involving 1,400 girls and women 14 to 45 years of age in the St Louis area, in which the use of LARC methods was promoted to reduce unintended pregnancy. Participants were educated about reversible contraception, with an emphasis on the benefits of LARC methods, and were provided with their choice

---

42 Ian Allen, 'Low take-up in contraception scheme,' *Marlborough Express* 21 February 2013.

of reversible contraception at no cost, and were followed for two to three years. The pregnancy, birth, and induced-abortion rates among teenage girls and women 15 to 19 years of age in this cohort were compared with those observed nationally among United States teens in the same age group. During the 2008-2013 period, the mean annual rates of pregnancy, birth, and abortion among CHOICE participants were 34, 19, and 10 per 1,000 teens, respectively. In comparison, rates of pregnancy, birth, and abortion among sexually experienced teens in the United States in 2008 were 159, 94 and 42 per 1000, respectively, which is an impressive result (Secura, 2014, 1316). Why the St Louis experiment worked well and that of New Zealand did not is not clear.

Family caps

About half of all states in the United States use family 'caps'. Family caps end the traditional system of welfare benefits that increase with family size and instead freeze the amount of a family's welfare grant at a level correlated to the number of children in the family at the time that the family began receiving assistance. Although the caps have their critics (Smith, 2006), it is arguable that limiting income puts the welfare household in the same situation as that of a working family, which does not automatically receive a wage increase every time it produces another child. The evidence suggests that the impact in non-marital birth rates is not consistent across all the target groups. One study of never-married mothers shows no evidence that family caps had an effect on subsequent childbearing but did not measure the effect on married mothers (Wallace, 2009, 73).

The Cameron Government in the United Kingdom announced a cap system in its first Budget following re-election in 2015. The Budget limits support provided to families through tax credits (and other benefits) to two children, so that any subsequent children born after April 2017 would not be eligible for further support (HM Treasury, 2015, 1.146). The experiment in the United Kingdom will be worth watching, however, there is every chance that family caps may not work because scarcity dictates that people under pressure make poor decisions. People may continue to have children and realise too late that money will not be forthcoming. Incentives and disincentives need to be immediate in their effect, so the delay in the impact may render the intervention less effective. Clearly, compliance is a problem, but if it is possible to use financial incentives to gain the same result then so be it. How much incentive will it take?

Behavioural economists ran an experiment in 2010 in one of Chicago's poorer areas, where they paid parents, whose names were drawn by lot, US$7,000 per year to have their child attend a pre-school (Gneezy, 2013, 99). One hundred and fifty children won the lottery, and attended. The parents also had to attend school, in this case a parent's academy. The researchers wanted to solve the problem at both ends, the child and the parenting. The effect of parental involvement and the impact of early childhood investment are bearing some fruit, but it is too early to tell if the improved results in the children's early years persist. It would be good if they did. The issues are, who could afford a scheme to be rolled out across a nation? The winners were chosen by lot, so what happens when others want a chance to win? How is a cut-off chosen so as to not draw in those who do not need assistance? Granted, this is not the researchers problem. It is their job to prove that incentives when well applied can have a significant impact, but it is the job of policy-makers who have to raise funds to pay for the incentives.

There is fascinating work on incentives and behaviour, which suggests that with the right incentives and obligations those who would otherwise fail may succeed. Whether these experiments prove to be applicable is debatable, but importantly the idea that enhancing the obligations expected of those on welfare is absolutely worth a trial. Many Australian women choose to have children, or are forced to have children, when they are on a benefit. The Government should not act as the father. It should rather act as friend and wise counsel, and have them delay pregnancy until they are in a stronger position to do so.

Bibliography

Abigail, W., Power, C., & Belan, I. (2008). Changing patterns in women seeking terminations of pregnancy: a trend analysis of data from one service provider 1996-2006. *Australian and New Zealand Journal of Public Health, 32*(3), 230–237.

Augustine, J. M., Nelson, T., & Edin, K. (2009). Why do poor men have children? Fertility intentions among low-income unmarried U.S. fathers. *The Annals of the American Academy of Political and Social Science, 624*(1), 99–117.

Australian Bureau of Statistics. (2003). *Breastfeeding in Australia, 2001.* Canberra.

Australian Bureau of Statistics. (2008). *How many children have women in Australia had?* Canberra.

Australian Bureau of Statistics. (2011). *Family characteristics, Australia, 2009-10.* Canberra.

Australian Bureau of Statistics (a). (2014). *Marriages and divorces, Australia, 2013.* Canberra.

Australian Bureau of Statistics (b). (2014). *Births, Australia, 2013.* Canberra.

Australian Bureau of Statistics (a). (2015). *Family characteristics and transitions, Australia, 2012-13.* Canberra.

Australian Bureau of Statistics (b). (2015). *Household and family projections, Australia 2011-36.* Canberra.

Australian Government. (2015). *Better tax system, better Australia.* Canberra: The Treasury.

Australian Institute of Health and Welfare (a). (2014). *Adoptions Australia 2013-14.* Canberra.

Australian Institute of Health and Welfare (b). (2014). *Child protection Australia 2012-13.* Canberra.

Australian Treasury. (2015). *Budget strategy and outlook budget paper no. 1.* Canberra: The Treasury.

Bachiochi, E. (2013). Women, sexual asymmetry, and Catholic teaching. *Christian Bioethics, 19*(2), 150–171.

Barón, J. D., Cobb-Clark, D., & Erkal, N. (2008). Cultural transmission of work-welfare attitudes and the intergenerational correlation in welfare receipt. *IZA Discussion Papers, No. 3904.*

Bartholomae, S. (2004). The legacy of welfare: economic endowments or cultural characteristics? *Journal of Family Issues, 25*(6), 783–810.

Black, K., Haber, P., & Lintzeris, N. (2012). Offering incentives to drug-using women to take up contraception: the ethical and clinical issues. *Addiction, 107*, 1361–1362.

Black, K. I., Bateson, D., & Harvey, C. (2013). Australian women need increased access to long-acting reversible contraception. *Medical Journal of Australia, 199*(September), 317–318.

Bor, W., McGee, T. R., & Fagan, A. A. (2004). Early risk factors for adolescent antisocial behaviour: an Australian longitudinal study. *The Australian and New Zealand Journal of Psychiatry, 38*, 365–372.

Boudreaux, C. J. (2014). Jumping off of the Great Gatsby curve: how institutions facilitate entrepreneurship and intergenerational mobility. *Journal of Institutional Economics, 10*(2), 231–255.

Bradshaw, C. J. A., & Brook, B. W. (2014). Human population reduction is not a quick fix for environmental problems. *Proceedings of the National Academy of Sciences, 111*(46), 16610–16615.

Brandon, P. D., & Fisher, G. A. (2001). The dissolution of joint living arrangements among single parents and children: does welfare make a difference? *Social Science Quarterly, 82*(1), 1–19.

Brown, S., & Guthrie, K. (2010). Why don't teenagers use contraception? A qualitative interview study. *The European Journal of Contraception & Reproductive Health Care, 15*(June), 197–204.

Byrne, L. K., Cook, K. E., Skouteris, H., & Do, M. (2011). Parental status and childhood obesity in Australia. *International Journal of Pediatric Obesity, 6*, 415–418.

Carbone, J., & Cahn, N. (2014). *Marriage markets: how inequality is remaking the American family* (Electronic.). New York: Oxford University Press.

Carmichael, G. (2014). Non-marital pregnancy and the second demographic transition in Australia in historical perspective. *Demographic Research, 30*(March), 609–640.

Causa, O. O., & Johansson, Å. (2010). Intergenerational social mobility in OECD Countries. *OECD Journal: Economic Studies, 2010*, 33–76.

Children's Court of Queensland. (2014). SB v Department of Communities & Ors. *QChC 7*.

Children's Court of Victoria. (2007). DOHS v Mr & Mrs B, *Vol. VChC 1*.

Children's Court of Victoria. (2008). DOHS v Mr D & Ms B, *Vol. VChC 2*.

Children's Court of Victoria (a). (2009). DOHS v Mr D & Ms W, *Vol. VChC 1*.

Children's Court of Victoria (b). (2009). TW, DOHS and P, F & R children, *Vol. VChC 6*.

Children's Court of Victoria (c). (2009). DOHS v Ms K & Mr L, *Vol. VChC 3*.

Children's Court of Victoria Family Division. (2013). K siblings, *Vol. VChC 1*.

Children's Court of Western Australia in Criminal. (2012). State of Western Australia v R, *Vol. WACC 1*.

Clark, G. (2014). *The son also rises: surnames and the history of social mobility* (Electronic.). New Jersey: Princeton University Press.

Cobb-Clark, D. (2010). Disadvantage across the generations. *Insights, 8*, 45–49.

Cobb-Clark, D., Ryan, C., & Sartbayeva, A. (2009). *Taking chances: the effect that growing up on welfare has on the risky behavior of young people. Youth in Focus Project Discussion Paper Series*. Canberra.

Cobb-Clark, D., & Sartbayeva, A. (2010). *The relationship between income-support history and the characteristics and outcomes of Australian youth. Youth in Focus Project Discussion Paper Series*. Canberra.

Cortis, N., Katz, I., & Patulney, R. (2009). *Engaging hard-to-reach families and children*. Canberra: Department of Families, Housing, Community Services and Indigenous Affairs.

Court of Protection UK. Re DD *EWCOP* (4) (Sterilisation) (2015).

Daraganova, G., & Thornton, L. (2013). Eating behaviour: socio-economic determinants and parental influence. *Longitudinal Study of Australian Children Annual Statistical Report 2013*, 91–110.

Department of Employment. (2014). *Job seeker compliance data: December quarter 2014*. Canberra: Commonwealth of Australia.

Department of Human Services (b). (2015). *Activity test/participation requirements.* Canberra: Centrelink.

Department of Social Services. (2014). *Income support customers: a statistical overview 2013.* Canberra.

Drago, R., Sawyer, K., Shreffler, K. M., Warren, D., & Wooden, M. (2011). Did Australia's baby bonus increase fertility intentions and births? *Population Research and Policy Review, 30,* 381–397.

Dulleck, U., Silva-Goncalves, J., & Torgler, B. (2014). *Impact evaluation of an incentive program on educational achievement of indigenous students.* Zurich: Center for Research in Economics, Management and the Arts.

Duncan, G. J., Magnuson, K., Kalil, A., & Ziol-Guest, K. (2012). The importance of early childhood poverty. *Social Indicators Research, 108,* 87–98.

Edwards, B., & Mullan, K. (2014). *The stronger families in Australia study: phase 2.* Melbourne: Australian Institute of Family Studies.

Evans, A. (2000). Power and negotiation: young women's choices about sex and contraception. *Journal of Population Research, 2,* 143–162.

Family Court of Australia. (2007). Davis v Davis and Another, *38 Fam LR.*

Family Court of Australia. (2012). Director-General, Department of Family and Community Services & Sheward and Ors, *FamCA 279.*

Family Court of Australia (a). (2014). Zanda v Zanda, *51 Fam LR.*

Family Court of Australia (b). (2014). Stonelake v Verboom, *FamCA 434.*

Family Court of Australia (a). (2015). Snell & Snell & Ors, *FamCA 420.*

Family Court of Australia (b). (2015). Scriven & Scriven & Ors, *FamCA 182.*

Federal Circuit Court of Australia. (2014). Drake & Drake & Anor, *FCCA 2950.*

Federal Office of Road Safety. (1985). *Fitting and wearing of seat belts in Australia: the history of a successful countermeasure.* Canberra.

Finer, L. B., & Zolna, M. R. (2014). Shifts in intended and unintended pregnancies in the United States, 2001-2008. *American Journal of Public Health, 104*(S1), 43–49.

Folbre, N., & Wolf, D. (2012). The intergenerational welfare state. *Population and*

Development Review, 38(Supplement), 36–51.

Gneezy, U., & List, J. (2013). *The why axis: hidden motives and the undicovered economics of everday life* (Electronic.). London: Random House.

Goodwin, V., & Davis, B. (2011). Crime families: gender and the intergenerational transfer of criminal tendencies. *Australian Institute of Criminology: Trends and Issues,* (414), 1–6.

Gray, E., & Evans, A. (2008). The limitations of understanding multi-partner fertility in Australia. *People and Place, 16*(4), 1–8.

Griffin, J. (2000). Welfare rights. *Journal of Ethics, 4,* 27–43.

Halford, W. K. I. M., & Simons, M. (2005). Couple relationship education in Australia. *Family Process, 44*(2), 147–159.

Hancock, K., Edwards, B., & Zubrick, S. R. (2012). Echoes of disadvantage across the generations? The influence of long-term joblessness and separation of grandparents on grandchildren. *Longitudinal Study of Australian Children Annual Statistical Report 2012,* 43–57.

Heard, G., & Dharmalingham, A. (2011). Socioeconomic differences in family formation: recent Australian trends. *New Zealand Population Review, 37,* 125–143.

Herscovitch, A., & Stanton, D. (2008). History of social security in Australia. *Family Matters,* (80), 51–60.

HM Treasury. (2015). *Summer Budget 2015.* London: House of Commons.

House of Representatives Standing Committee on Social and Legal Affairs. (2015). *From conflict to cooperation: inquiry into the child support program.* Canberra: The Parliament of the Commonwealth of Australia.

Jeon, S. H., Kalb, G., & Vu, H. (2011). The dynamics of welfare participation among women who experienced teenage motherhood in Australia. *Economic Record, 87*(277), 235–251.

Jones, R. K., & Dreweke, J. (2011). *Countering conventional wisdom: new evidence on religion and contraceptive use.* New York: Guttmacher Institute.

Layte, R., McGee, H., Rundle, K., & Leigh, C. (2007). Does ambivalence about becoming pregnant explain social class differentials in use of contraception? *European Journal of Public Health, 17*(5), 477–482.

Lindberg, L. D., & Maddow-Zimet, I. (2012). Consequences of sex education on teen and young adult sexual behaviors and outcomes. *Journal of Adolescent Health*, *51*(4), 332–338.

Liu, P. Y., Swerdloff, R. S., Christenson, P. D., Handelsman, D. J., & Wang, C. (2006). Rate, extent, and modifiers of spermatogenic recovery after hormonal male contraception: an integrated analysis. *Lancet*, *367*, 1412–1420.

Lohiya, N. K., Alam, I., Hussain, M., Khan, S. R., & Ansari, A. S. (2014). RISUG: an intravasal injectable male contraceptive. *Indian Journal of Medical Research*, *140*(Supplement), 63–72.

Lucke, J. C., & Hall, W. D. (2012). Under what conditions is it ethical to offer incentives to encourage drug-using women to use long-acting forms of contraception? *Addiction*, *107*, 1036–1041.

Lynn, R. (2001). *Eugenics: a reassessment*. London: Praeger.

Maher, M. J., Sever, L. M., & Pichler, S. (2007). Beliefs versus lived experience: gender differences in Catholic college students' attitudes concerning premarital sex and contraception. *American Journal of Sexuality Education*, *2*(4), 67–87.

Marie Stopes International. (2006). *What women want: when faced with an unplanned pregnancy*. Melbourne.

Marshall, J. M., Huang, H., & Ryan, J. P. (2011). Intergenerational families in child welfare: assessing needs and estimating permanency. *Children and Youth Services Review*, *33*, 1024–1030.

Martinelli, C., & Parker, S. (2003). Should transfers to poor families be conditional on school attendance? A household bargaining prespective. *International Economic Review*, *44*(2), 523–544.

Mazza, D., Harrison, C., Taft, A., Brijnath, B., Britt, H., Hobbs, M., … Hussainy, S. (2012). Current contraceptive management in Australian general practice: an analysis of BEACH data. *Medical Journal of Australia*, *197*(2), 110–114.

McArthur, M., Thomson, L., & Winkworth, G. (2013). Jumping through hoops: the cost of compliance on sole parents. *Child and Family Social Work*, *18*, 159–167.

McArthur, M., & Winkworth, G. (2013). The hopes and dreams of Australian young mothers in receipt of income support. *Communities, Children and Families Australia*, *7*(1), 47–62.

McHugh, M., & Bell, A. (2013). *Reforming the foster care system in Australia*. Sydney: Berry Street.

McLachlan, R., Gilfillan, G., & Gordon, J. (2013). *Deep and persistent disadvantage in Australia*. Canberra: Productivity Commission.

McLanahan, S. (2004). Diverging destinies: how children are faring under the second demographic transition. *Demography, 41*(4), 607–627.

Meriggiola, M. C., & Pelusi, G. (2014). Advances in male hormonal contraception. *Indian Journal of Medical Research, 140*(Supplement), 58–62.

Miller, A. R., & Zhang, L. (2012). Intergenerational effects of welfare reform on educational attainments. *Journal of Law and Economics, 55*(2), 437–476.

Mistler, G., Kirkwood, K., Potter, E., & Cashin, A. (2008). Young offenders in New South Wales, Australia and the need for remedial sexual health education. *Sex Education, 8*(4), 439–449.

Mullainathan, S., & Shafir, E. (2015). *Scarcity: the true cost of having nothing* (Electronic.). Penguin.

Mullan, K., & Higgins, D. (2014). *A safe and supportive family environment for children: key components and links to child outcomes*. Canberra: Department of Social Services.

Murray, C. (2013). *Coming apart: the state of white America 1960-2010* (Electronic.). New York: Crowne Forum.

New Zealand House of Representatives Health Committee. (2013). *Inquiry into improving child health outcomes and preventing child abuse, with a focus on pre-conception until three years of age*. Wellington.

New Zealand Ministry for Social Development (a). (2012). *Cabinet papers and regulatory impact statements: welfare reform paper A – overview*. Wellington.

New Zealand Ministry for Social Development (b). (2012). *Cabinet papers and regulatory impact statements: welfare reform paper C – parents on a benefit who have subsequent children*. Wellington.

Nowak, C., & Heinrichs, N. (2008). A comprehensive meta-analysis of triple P-positive parenting program using hierarchical linear modeling: effectiveness and moderating variables. *Clinical Child and Family Psychology Review, 11*(3), 114–144.

Ong, J., Temple-Smith, M., Wong, W. C. W., McNamee, K., & Fairley, C. (2012).

Contraception matters: indicators of poor usage of contraception in sexually active women attending family planning clinics in Victoria, Australia. *BMC Public Health, 12*(1108), 1–10.

Ong, J., Temple-Smith, M., Wong, W., McNamee, K., & Fairley, C. (2013). Prevalence of and characteristics associated with use of withdrawal among women in Victoria, Australia. *Perspectives on Sexual and Reproductive Health, 45*(2), 74–77.

Parr, N. (2006). Do children from small families do better? *Journal of Population Research, 23*(1), 1–25.

Parr, N., & Guest, R. (2011). The contribution of increases in family benefits to Australia's early 21st-century fertility increase: an empirical analysis. *Demographic Research, 25*, 215–244.

Pech, J., & McCoull, F. (2000). Transgenerational welfare dependence: myths and realities. *Australian Social Policy, 1*, 43–67.

Pedersen, W. (2011). Cannabis and social welfare assistance: a longitudinal study. *Addiction, 106*, 1636–1643.

Perelli-Harris, B., Berrington, A., Berghammer, C., Keizer, R., Lappegård, T., Mynarska, M., ... Vignoli, D. (2014). Towards a new understanding of cohabitation. *Demographic Research, 31*, 1043–1078.

Productivity Commission (a). (2015). *Report on government services*. Canberra.

Productivity Commission (b). (2015). *Tax and transfer incidence in Australia*. Canberra.

Queensland Child Protection Commission of Inquiry. (2013). *Taking responsibility: a roadmap for Queensland child protection*. Brisbane.

Rassi, A., Wattimena, J., & Black, K. (2013). Pregnancy intention in an urban Australian antenatal population. *Australian and New Zealand Journal of Public Health, 37*(6), 568–573.

Rebstock, P. (2011). *Reducing long-term benefit dependency. Welfare Working Group*. Wellington: Victoria University.

Reeve, R., & van Gool, K. (2013). Modelling the relationship between child abuse and long-term health care costs and wellbeing: results from an Australian community-based survey. *Economic Record, 89*(286), 300–318.

Reference Group on Welfare Reform to the Minister for Social Services. (2015).

A new system for better employment and social outcomes. Canberra.

Risse, L. (2010). "... And one for the country" The effect of the baby bonus on Australian women's childbearing intentions. *Journal of Population Research, 27*(3), 213–240.

Salter, F. K. (2015). Eugenics, ready or not. *Quadrant*, (May-June).

Sammut, J. (2015). *The madness of Australian child protection: why adoption will rescue Australia's underclass children.* Ballarat: Connor Court.

Sawhill, I. (2014). *Generation unbound: drifting into sex and parenthood without marriage* (Electronic.). Wahington DC: Brookings Institution Press.

Secura, G. M., Madden, T., McNicholas, C., Mullersman, J., Buckel, C. M., Zhao, Q., & Peipert, J. F. (2014). Provision of no-cost, long-acting contraception and teenage pregnancy. *The New England Journal of Medicine, 371*(14), 1316–1323.

Segal, L., & Dalziel, K. (2011). Investing to protect our children: using economics to derive an evidence-based strategy. *Child Abuse Review, 20*(May), 274–289.

Shaw, M., Lawlor, D. A., & Najman, J. M. (2006). Teenage children of teenage mothers: psychological, behavioural and health outcomes from an Australian prospective longitudinal study. *Social Science and Medicine, 62*(10), 2526–2539.

Sinclair, S., Boymal, J., & De Silva, A. (2012). A re-appraisal of the fertility response to the Australian baby bonus. *Economic Record, 88*(Special Issue), 78–87.

Smith, R. J. (2006). Family caps in welfare reform: their coercive effects and damaging consequences. *Harvard Journal of Law and Gender, 29*, 151–200.

State Coroner Queensland (a). (2015). *Inquest into the death of A, a 6 year old child.*

State Coroner Queensland (b). (2015). *Inquest into the deaths of JE and JJ.*

State Coroner South Australia. (2014). *Inquest into the death of Chloe Lee Valentine.*

Stephens, M. (2013). Seeking the common good or just making us be good? Recent amendment to New Zealand's social security law. *Victoria University of Wellington Law Review, 44*, 383–402.

Stoddard, A., McNicholas, C., & Peipert, J. F. (2011). Efficacy and safety of long-acting reversible contraception. *Drugs, 71*(8), 969–980.

Thomson, E., Lappegård, T., Carlson, M., Evans, A., & Gray, E. (2014). Childbearing across partnerships in Australia, the United States, Norway, and Sweden. *Demography, 51*, 485–508.

Tucker, J. S., Sussell, J., Golinelli, D., Zhou, A., Kennedy, D. P., & Wenzel, S. L. (2012). Understanding pregnancy-related attitudes and behaviors: a mixed-methods study of homeless youth. *Perspectives on Sexual and Reproductive Health, 44*(4), 252–61.

Vartanian, T. P., & McNamara, J. M. (2004). The welfare myth: disentangling the long-term effects of poverty and welfare receipt for young single mothers. *Journal of Sociology & Social Welfare, 31*(4), 105–140.

Victorian Civil and Administrative Tribunal. (2015). TRV v Department of Health and Human Services, *VCAT 1188*.

Visser, R. O. De, Smith, A. M. A., Richters, J., & Rissel, C. E. (2007). Associations between religiosity and sexuality in a representative sample of Australian adults. *Archives of Sexual Behavior, 36*(1), 33–46.

Wallace, G. L. (2009). The effects of family caps on the subsequent fertility decisions of never-married mothers. *Journal of Population Research, 26*(1), 73–101.

Walsh, J. (2013). Let's talk sex. *HIV Australia, 11*(1), 37–38.

Weaver, H., Smith, G., & Kippax, S. (2005). School-based sex education policies and indicators of sexual health among young people: a comparison of the Netherlands, France, Australia and the United States. *Sex Education, 5*(2), 171–188.

Weston, R., & Qu, L. (2014). *Trends in family transitions, forms and functioning.* Melbourne: Australian Institute of Family Studies.

Wilkins, R. (2014). *Statistical report on waves 1 to 11 of the household, income and labour dynamics in Australia survey.* Melbourne: Melbourne Institute of Applied Economic and Social Research.

Wolf, A. (2013). *The XX factor: how working women are creating a new society* (Electronic.). London: Profile Books.

Index